HOW TO
STOP
DRINKING
ALCOHOL

A Simple Path from Alcohol Misery to Alcohol Mastery

BY
KEVIN O'HARA

For Sean
I'm so proud to be your dad x

How to Stop Drinking Alcohol

This book is not intended as a substitute for the medical advice of physicians. The reader should regularly consult a physician in matters relating to his/her health and particularly with respect to any symptoms that may require diagnosis or medical attention.

Second edition, 2015

Stihlman Publishing
Rojales
Alicante

ISBN-13: 978-1512238761

ISBN-10:1512238767

Contents

Introduction

"Habit, my friend, is practice long pursued, that at last becomes man himself."
Evenus

Journey's Beginning

Welcome to *How to Stop Drinking Alcohol.*

It's amazing to me now, looking back at all my years as a drinker, that I never saw a problem with what I was doing to myself or to those around me. I started drinking alcohol back in the late 1970s and I stopped at the beginning of 2013. In all that time, right up until I finally quit, I never thought I would stop drinking or that I would ever want to stop.

Then when I did realize that I had a problem, I automatically thought that there was something wrong with me personally. I thought that I was just one of those people who couldn't handle alcohol. That line of thinking did not come about by accident. Reasoning that I was an alcoholic, that I probably had an addictive brain, and that there was very little I could do about it is an integral part of our alcohol consuming culture. I had been programmed to think that way and that programming had started from the day I was born.

The truth is that every alcohol drinker has been captured by the same programming. We always think about the propaganda of alcohol use coming exclusively from the alcohol companies. In fact, they have a very simple job to do in convincing us to take up the habit. By the time we get to taking our first sip of alcohol, we are already well and truly hooked into the alcohol culture. The addiction to this drug has been slowly brewing from the day you were born. We will look at this in much more detail throughout this book.

Now that I have stopped drinking alcohol, I'm loving every minute of it. With all my doubts and anxieties about a life without alcohol, once the programming was revealed and I saw alcohol drinking for what it was, a very destructive drug habit, quitting turned out to be very simple.

Quitting alcohol is extremely liberating. Your whole life will change remarkably when you alter your alcohol perceptions and see what destruction your alcohol use has been causing in your life. That's the essence of what this book is about. With that in mind, there's every reason to start your journey feeling very happy about your decision to quit.

Feeling Happy About Your Decision

Why should you feel happy about giving something up? Because you are not giving anything up, you are eliminating a deadly substance from your life. This drug is a toxin. Every single drop you drink contaminates your body and your mind. Alcohol represses your relationships, work life, home life, and sex life. Drinking this toxin corrupts your perceptions about yourself and about the world around you.

Furthermore, the blind acceptance of alcohol as a 'normal' part of a healthy life contaminates the thinking of the next generation and perpetuates this dangerous habit into the future. When we use alcohol around our children, we tell them that there is nothing wrong with it, that it's not drug use, and that they should follow on in our footsteps when they reach adulthood.

The drinks industry would have you believe that there is such a thing as responsible drinking. Can there ever be anything responsible about deliberately consuming a poison, even in the pursuit of happiness?

The moment you stop drinking is the moment you get to make a fresh start. That is a cause for real celebration.

5% Alcohol

How to Stop Drinking Alcohol will show you that <u>your addiction to alcohol is mostly an illusion</u>. Like a pint of average strength beer, quitting drinking is only 5% about the alcohol. The other 95% involves making the changes to those parts of your life that have supported your alcohol drinking habit. If you choose to be an alcoholic for the rest of your life, that is exactly what you will be! All you have to do is to keep thinking that you are an alcoholic. However, if you want to lead a life that does not rely on a drug to get you through the day, you can do that as well.

You don't need to hide from alcohol for the remainder of your days. Far from it. This book will show you how alcohol is a dangerous drug with no part to play in a healthy or natural life.

Life Long Disinformation

You will learn about the propaganda that keeps you thinking about alcohol, even when you know drinking is not good for you.

We will look at how your everyday language can affect how you see things. We'll examine your use of words like alcoholic, moderation, recovery, and the demon drink. We will also take a close look at your expectations of the symptoms and side effects of quitting drinking. I will show you some simple tricks to alter your thinking and your entire alcohol quitting experience.

I will show you that your fears can hurt you before you even start on your journey and how making some small changes will allow you to step across your starting line full of confidence about the road ahead.

Finally, we will examine what you should realistically expect once you quit. Thankfully most of us don't have to sign ourselves into a dry out clinic, spending the price of a small house into the bargain. Most of us can quit drinking alcohol on our own.

You Are Not Alone

There are millions of people who have already stopped drinking alcohol without the need for professional intervention. They did not need to be admitted to hospital, they did not experience serious side effects or symptoms, and they stopped taking this drug without feeling any intense cravings to ever drink alcohol again.

From my experience, and from the experiences of millions of others who have stopped drinking permanently, quitting alcohol is mostly in the mind. If you can control your thoughts, you control your actions.

Speak To Your Doctor

Before we go further into this book, I would advise anyone who is about to embark on this wonderful journey to visit their doctor first. Have a chat with them and let them know what your plans are. They'll be only too happy to hear your great news and you are better being safe than sorry.

Chapter One - It's Time to Stop!

"To study the abnormal is the best way of understanding the normal."
William James

Daily Dosing

I don't know exactly when it was that I started drinking every day. I had reached the stage where I found it hard to relax without a few cans of beer or a bottle or two of wine. I started to need alcohol to do the normal everyday things like sleep. I never had problems sleeping when I was young; now I *had* to drink or I would be tossing and turning for most of the night.

I often took a day off from alcohol, maybe two if I could manage. I had to prove to myself that I could stay away from the booze. I wanted to displace any fears that I was turning into an alcoholic. My logic was really simple, if you are an alcoholic you cannot go even one day without a drink. Therefore if I could last a day or two without alcohol, even if it was only once in a blue moon, it was proof that I had it all under control and I was capable of handling my drinking.

Why Stop Now?

What finally made me want to stop?

There are so many reasons why someone will decide that enough is enough. This decision never comes easily. Normally, just like in my case, the push to quit comes after a lot of denying that there is even a problem. But eventually there comes a time when you start to weigh up your life. You clearly see that this is not what you expected. This was not the place you thought you would end up.

The Catalysts

Maybe you have had a health scare. You are feeling a pain in the liver that scares the crap out of you. A visit to the family doctor brings some worrying 'home truths'. Or it is dawning on you that you are just not feeling that great any more.

Maybe your hangovers are lasting more than a day, maybe even stretching into two or three days. You might have reached the stage where the hangovers are becoming unbearable. Do need to have a drink during the day just to feel some relief, just to feel "normal"?

Are you experiencing problems in your relationships? Perhaps your husband or wife is saying that they just can't stand it anymore. An ultimatum has been presented to you - either the alcohol goes or the relationship.

Have you gotten in trouble with the law? Your catalyst could have happened after being stopped by the police while you were drunk behind the wheel of your car. You were loaded with a big fine, you lost your license, and you have to put up with the shame of standing in front of a packed court house while the judge issues your sentence!

Your Personal Tipping Point

In most cases there will be just the one catalyzing event. This event will not necessarily be earth shattering in its impact. The same situation might even have happened before, maybe even many times. But this time is different. Now you can feel the full force of the impact and it is changing the way you think about your drinking.

Your personal tipping point might be just one in a long line of incidents and happenings, but this is the one event that finally opens your eyes to the life you are living and what you have to look forward to if you don't stop using alcohol.

DUI and Ten Months Off

That is just the way it was for me when I stopped drinking in 2008. I was pulled over by the police in December 2007 after leaving a pub and jumping into my car for the short spin home. I was breathalyzed on the spot, arrested, handcuffed, taken to the police station, and charged with drinking and driving.

After the embarrassment of appearing in court, I was fined heavily and my license was suspended for a year. Things could have been much worse. I still think about how lucky I was to have been stopped that night. It was the wakeup call I needed to catalyze my brain into action.

Thankfully, there was no real long term damage done. I paid the fine, learned a very valuable lesson, and moved on with my life. Although I didn't quit for good at that time, the whole mess paved the way for my decision to quit alcohol permanently, five years later.

I stopped drinking before I appeared in court and I didn't start again for ten months. Those ten months gave me the belief in myself that I could quit drinking long term. It took another five years, many other individual incidents and accidents, and one final catalyzing moment in late 2012, before I could finally motivate my pickled brain to take action.

New Life

How did I know it was time to finally stop using this drug for good?

My partner Esther and I moved to Spain in 2011. We had many reasons for wanting to make the move. For a start there was the change in pace. I had been working in forestry for over ten years and the damp Irish climate was beginning to take its toll on my joints. There was also the change of scenery, with the year-round sun of Alicante playing a huge part.

Near the top of the list of personal reasons, although I didn't broadcast this one too widely, was all the cheap booze. It's funny because I was even hiding that reason from myself. If you had come up to me in the months before we moved and asked me why we were going, I would not have mentioned booze. At least it would have been near the bottom. But as soon as we arrived at our new Spanish home, wine was one of the first things we bought, and lots of it!

We made our plans, packed our stuff, and finally drove for the ferry in late November 2012. Despite lots of appealing from me, my son wanted to stay put in Ireland. Leaving him on the last day was heart-wrenching for me at the time. In retrospect, it was something that was good for both of us. Being on his own gave him independence and self-belief. He kept pointing out to me that it was only a short flight to Spain and we could speak to each other via Skype all the time.

Fun in the Sun

Anyway, long story short, we moved to Spain and I saw Sean when he came over on holidays. It made no sense for me to make the journey back to Ireland, it was way cheaper for him to come here. Even though I spoke to him three or four times a week, I still missed him a lot, and I wanted to see him as much as possible.

Of course, once he was here, we wanted to have as much fun as possible. I'd save up some money and once he got here I'd take a week or two off work. As I've already mentioned, fun to me has always involved drinking lots of alcohol and Sean coming over on vacation was no exception.

I never stopped to think about the message I was sending to him through my behavior, the example that I was setting. Of course being a bad influence was always present in the back of my mind, but like anything else in my life, the solution to most problems or negative thoughts was to get drunk.

The Final Straw!

By Christmas of 2012, I hadn't seen Sean for a few months, so I was really looking forward to seeing him and having a good time over the holiday season.

A few days after he'd arrived, my partner Esther was working in the evening so Sean and I went out on the town for a pub crawl. I can't remember exactly when we started drinking. More than likely we drank a few beers on the balcony before we left home. Towards the end of the night, we arrived at a local Scottish "Celtic" bar.

We settled in and had a few rounds. Toward closing time, I ran out of money, and I knew Sean still had five euros in his pocket. I asked him would he lend it to me until we got home. He refused. We got into a stupid argument which didn't last that long. Sean eventually bought the last round, and we left the bar laughing. The incident meant nothing in the grand scheme of things and I really should have forgotten about it altogether. But for some reason it stuck in my head and wouldn't be shaken.

I couldn't get rid of the feeling that I was being a complete louse. I couldn't believe that I'd pulled a fight with my son just so I could have one more pint to add to the 15 or 20 I'd already drank. I think that for the first time I really started to think about the damage I was doing to his life by inadvertently encouraging him to use alcohol.

Once Sean had gone back to Ireland, everything hit me hard. It was a mixture of seeing him off at the airport, not knowing when I would see him again, and a growing shame I about my role as a father. I felt as if the entire two weeks had just been wasted. Instead of great memories of a fantastic holiday, I remember drinking, eating, hangovers, and *that* argument.

Finally, I could see how much I was wasting my life.

It was my time to stop!

The First Time I Ever Drank

"In youth we learn; in age we understand."
Marie von Ebner-Eschenbach

It has been a long time since I took my first drink of alcohol. I was 13 or 14 and, from what I can remember, the main reason I started to drink was because I desperately wanted to grow up. I didn't feel like a boy, I felt a man; the problem was that nobody else could see it.

My best mate at the time was another plastic paddy like myself. Although his real name was Paul, everyone knew him as Molly because of the huge mop of rusty curly hair. I don't know where he got the nickname from, I suppose from Molly Malone.

During one of those long hot Irish summers (at least that's how I remember it!), Molly and I built a rickety shed in my back garden. We made it from old bits of wood, long strips of rusted corrugated sheeting, odd bricks, bits of plastic, and lots of cardboard. We christened it "The Secret Headquarters" and it was the place where we made our plans to conquer the world.

Try Beer - Get Drunk

One of our first plans involved getting some beer and hopefully getting drunk. First we had to get our parents to agree to the two of us spending the night in the garden, unsupervised. That wasn't an easy thing. We were a pair of true tearaways, getting into trouble at the drop of a hat. With a lot of pleading and a whole pot of promises, we secured the approval. Now all we had to do was buy the beer, wait until everyone was in bed, and begin our boozy experiment.

I can't remember where we got the money for the beer. We probably pinched it from our trusting parents.

Our plan was simple. We'd wait outside the local pub until we saw someone who we thought we could smooth talk, someone who's eyes we could pull the wool over. We would put on our best innocent faces, ask nicely, hand over the money, and hope for the best.

To our surprise and immense satisfaction, it worked first time.

We stopped this old guy who was just about to go into the pub. Looking back on it now with more experienced eyes, he must have known what we were up to before we even opened our mouths. Very politely, we asked if he wouldn't mind buying us a six pack of beer. We told him that it was for our Mum who was sick in bed and under doctor's orders to drink some beer.

What type of beer, he asked. We didn't know any brands, so we told him it didn't matter!

He went into the bar and we had no idea if that was the last we'd ever see of him.

After an anxious wait, he came back out. With a wink and a smile he handed us a brown paper bag. It felt heavy but I hugged that bag against my chest as if it contained the family jewels. We ran all the way back to the house, laughing our heads of and full of excitement about the adventure that lay ahead.

Ranking the Taste

I remember that first taste like it was yesterday. It was an Irish bitter called Smithwicks. I could not have chosen a more apt word for this muck if I had named it myself: Bitter by name, bitter by nature.

It was absolutely awful. The taste of that swill hitting the back of my tongue, and the feeling of trying to get it down my throat without gagging, were the things about that night that stick out most vividly in my memory.

I don't remember much after that first taste. I don't know if I got drunk on my three little bottles, if I threw up, if our escapades were uncovered by our parents, or how soon we tried to repeat the experience.

I know that this early drinking episode didn't exactly turn me into a raving fan, that's for sure. Even though I was still searching for ways to feel grown up, alcohol wasn't on the top of my list any more.

Unfortunately, the foul taste was not enough to put me off for life.

My Alcohol Use

"By three methods we may learn wisdom: First, by reflection, which is noblest; Second, by imitation, which is easiest; and third by experience, which is the bitterest."
Confucius

My alcohol use has followed a fairly predictable path over the years. It's a similar path to that which has been taken by many other drinkers. I bet you'll recognize a lot of what follows in your own life.

Like so many other users, even though my legal drinking career didn't start until bang on the day of my 18th birthday, the culture had taken care of the brainwashing a long time before I'd had my first sip. By the time I took that first sip, I was already well and truly hooked into the alcoholic culture. The stage was set for my many years of drug use right on the day I was born.

My Pre-Drinking Brainwashing

I was born in London, June 1966. That first birthday was also my first roundabout introduction to alcohol. My parents didn't stick a dram of whiskey into my feeding bottle or anything like that, but they did raise a few glasses of alcohol to wet my head. This tradition of wetting the baby's head is supposed celebrate the birth and welcome the infant into the family and the wider world. In reality, it's the chance for the parents, or more likely the father, to go on a bender. Probably a few more bottles were cracked open when my mother brought me home from the hospital, and again when I was christened. Even the parish priest gets in on the act.

Though I wasn't consciously aware of it at the time, the seeds of my future alcohol habit were already being sown in my young brain.

Children learn mostly through imitating those around them. You are also heavily influenced by the place and time you were born. If you were born into the western culture in the 20th and 21st centuries, for instance, alcohol is going to be play a large part in your normal everyday life. The same processes would have dictated that if you happened to be a male born into an 8th century Viking family, raiding, raping, and pillaging would have been a 'normal' part of your life. Normalcy, in other words, is based on chance.

It was only in the early 20th century that opium was made illegal in most western countries. For many people, born while opium was legal, opium use may well have been considered 'normal'.

Adult Drinking

Throughout my childhood, and I'm sure the same applies to you, I saw adults drinking alcohol and never thought too much about it. That's just the way it was. My parents weren't alcoholics by any stretch of the imagination. They weren't even regular drinkers. My dad didn't go to the pub. And it was rare to see him drinking in the house.

My mum drank even less. A glass of wine was all it took to make her giggle like a schoolgirl. If she had more than one, she'd just act silly for hours. She used to smoke in the same take-it-or-leave-it fashion. She would normally make a pack of cigarettes last her for a week or more. My mum's addiction was her kids. She had 13 altogether, with nine surviving the womb. I don't think she ever had time to get drunk. In fact it was only later in life, once we'd all flown the nest, that I ever saw her drunk. She was one of the few real social drinkers I knew. She didn't really like drinking. But she would join in just to be involved, just to be sociable.

Like most homes, alcohol was used as a routine part of our family celebrations. There was more alcohol in our house at Christmas than at any other time during the year. I think my dad wanted to have a bottle of every imaginable alcoholic drink, just to make sure there was something for everyone who might turn up on the doorstep. It was a part of the tradition.

A Normal Upbringing

So we were raised with alcohol drinking as a normal part of life. As part of that normalcy, as a child you understand that alcohol is only available for the grown-ups. When you are very young, alcohol does not hold much interest. It's the smelly stuff that the grown-ups drink. When the grown-ups drink the smelly stuff they act very strange. The older you get, the more interesting alcohol becomes. You start to wonder *why* everyone is acting strange once they have been drinking. You start to wonder what it would be like to drink some alcohol. Words like drunk become a part of your vocabulary and you wonder what being drunk feels like. The closer you get to adulthood, the more significant alcohol becomes.

To be able to legally buy your own booze and drink it in a pub is one of the biggest cultural signals that you have finally reached adulthood. You have crossed into a different world of responsibility and using alcohol is one rite of passage that

I grew up in England* during the late 1960's and throughout the 70's. It was a bad time for work in the UK, and my dad finally decided to move us home to Ireland in 1978, just before I turned 12. I can't say that Ireland was any different to the UK in terms of alcohol use. Both countries have similar pub cultures, and they tend to use alcohol in much the same way.

During my teenage years in Dublin, there was a huge problem with heroin. At one point, 12% of 15 - 19 years olds in the city had used the drug over the previous year. To try and combat this, the government set up the Special Government Task Force on Drug Abuse which, like most of the ilk, failed abysmally. The task force concluded with a report which recommended creating and funding facilities in deprived communities. Because this went against government policies at the time, the report was ignored and never made public. Communities around the city responded to the crisis by forming groups of their own to try and deal with drug dealers. These groups involved ordinary residents, priests, and politicians. Some groups even involved members of the IRA. Many of these groups came together to form the Concerned Parents Against Drugs group. Many people died during that time, mostly from what was mixed in with street heroin to bulk it out, shared needles, and of course the violence that comes with illegal drugs.

Those deaths, the constant news reports, and the general fear about the drug itself definitely shied me away from ever touching the stuff. I never witnessed anyone taking heroin. Some of the kids in my school were sniffing glue or gas, but that just seemed like a stupid craze.

While we all feared heroin, the biggest drugs in the country, the biggest drug killers in the world, alcohol and cigarettes, were free to be sold to anyone who wanted to buy them. As you know, this is a situation that has not been resolved.

As a side note - in the UK it's legal to drink alcohol at home, or in any private premises, once you're over the age of 5. Check out this page from the British Citizen's Advice Bureau.

18 At Last!

By the time I reached my 18th birthday, I could finally buy my own supplies of alcohol. Not that I had not been drinking copious amounts before I was 'legal'. But by the age of 18, I was well and truly hooked into the binge drinking culture. I could not wait to get into a pub to order my first "grown up" pint. At 18, I could drink what I wanted, where I wanted, and when I wanted. I took every possible opportunity to indulge. I still had not "acquired" the taste for alcohol so my Guinness was served with blackcurrant flavoring and my lager with a dash of lime.

The only thing that held me back and stopped me from indulging too much was lack of money. Alcohol was expensive and my job didn't pay that much. So I only drank at the weekends. Depending on who was buying, and how cheaply we could buy our booze, the weekend could mean any time from Thursday to Sunday. It could mean a couple of pints after work, or an all-out binge drinking session that started on Friday and lasted through until the early hours of Monday morning. Many of those binging sessions would often end only when I was so drunk that I could hardly stand, talk, retain the contents of my stomach, or find my way home.

It has been discovered in recent years, through using MRI technology, that the human brain has not become fully developed by the time a person reaches the age of 18. In fact, the brain continues its development into the person's early 20's. One of the last parts of the brain to develop fully is the pre-frontal cortex, often called the CEO of the brain. This is the part of the brain which is responsible for decision making, problem solving, and reasoning. It's the part of the brain that holds back risky behavior and the desire for chasing after big thrills. It is this reasoning part of the brain that separates us from the beast. When an adolescent does drugs, including alcohol, it not only affects them in the next few hours or gives them a hangover the next day, it may also be affecting them for the rest of their lives.

Alcohol - The Tool

Since those first bottles of beer in my back garden, I have always used alcohol as a tool. It was widely available, legal, and its consumption was encouraged by almost everyone.

In the early days, I used alcohol as a way of blending in with the crowd, of being sociable, or to help me find the Dutch courage I needed to overcome my shyness when chatting up the girls. Later in life, I used alcohol as a relief from boredom, to escape pain, as a relaxant, or as a pick me up.
As I got older, and the after effects of my binge drinking sessions were hitting me harder, I used alcohol as "the hair of the dog," a way of masking the symptoms of the inevitable horrible hangover.

Behavior Modifier

This drug has been my default behavior modification tool whenever I have had any emotions I could not deal with. Instead of learning the skills and techniques to live my life and to deal with my problems, I have handled things by getting drunk. If I can't deal with a certain person, I'll get drunk. If I don't know how to manage myself in a particular situation, I'll have a couple of drinks and forget about the whole thing.

If in doubt, have a drink. If bored, have a drink. If tired, have a drink. If unsure, have a drink.

Eventually, drinking alcohol becomes the norm.

Just as a dog can be trained to salivate at the sound of a bell, so we can train ourselves to associate enjoyment, parties, fun, or celebration with drinking lots of alcohol. Enjoyment and alcohol evolve into constant companions, one becoming inseparable from the other.

Throughout my drinking life, I cannot remember ever spending a weekend without using alcohol. I stopped playing any sports as soon as I left school, unless I could play them while drinking. Alcohol was the reason I got very good at playing pool and throwing darts; they are both pub "sports" which I could play while slowly getting drunk. I could also drink while I watched other people playing sports. The pubs and bars are always packed on match day with people staring at the TV and packing away the pints.

Your Commitment to Quit

"Commitment is an act, not a word."
Jean-Paul Sartre

The one thing that will guarantee your success on this new journey is you making the full commitment to quit. If you are fully committed to never drinking alcohol again, how can you fail? You cannot!

The task of quitting drinking alcohol is simple, you simply refuse to allow another drop of alcohol to pass your lips, ever!

Every alcohol habit is built one mouthful of booze at a time. If you put a stop to the mouthfuls, you kill the source for the habit. Job done!

This is the only guaranteed way of stopping!

Everything else is simply about adjusting and learning how to live your life without alcohol. It's a process. It's a skill that you learn how to do, then you practice and practice until it becomes natural. This is exactly the same way you learned how to drink. You practiced drinking until it became second nature.

Cross the starting line with the mantra - *I'm done with alcohol, no more*!

And that's it.

Start now. Don't deviate.

Start now. Don't deviate.

Start now and never deviate.

Chapter Two - Alcohol in Our Culture

"What fascinates me about addiction and obsessive behavior is that people would choose an altered state of consciousness that's toxic and ostensibly destroys most aspects of your normal life, because for a brief moment you feel okay."
Moby

Facts About Alcohol Use In Our Culture

Alcohol is part of our culture, whether we like it or not, and it is not going to go anywhere fast. People are still going to consume alcohol whether we drink it or not, whether we like it or not, so we have to factor that into our overall plan for success.

Although other drugs are also a part of our culture, alcohol can be much more damaging because alcohol use is considered to be 'normal'. It's a 'normal' thing drink alcohol when we want to relax, have fun, celebrate, or when we want to mourn.

Not only is alcohol consumption treated as 'normal', not using this drug is often treated as 'abnormal'. This means that once you finally realize that alcohol is poisoning you and causing you harm, and you actually quit using it, only then are you regarded as having a problem.

In terms of harms to the individual and to the society in which we all live, alcohol comes out as one of the most damaging drugs being used today. A UK based study* looking at overall harm, has shown that alcohol is the most harmful drug by a wide margin. The study tested across 3 basic factors - physical, psychological, and social. There were 16 identified harm criteria which include drug specific mortality, drug related mortality, drug specific and related damage, dependence, loss of tangibles, loss of relationships, crime, and economic cost.

Big Alcohol

The alcohol industry, or Big Alcohol (BA), fosters the aim that alcohol should be accepted as a normal part of our cultures and societies. BA actively opposes any attempts to control the overall use of alcohol or to recatergorize alcohol as a drug. BA is largely self-regulated, and although they say that they have the best interests of you, the consumer, in mind, those interests will always be subordinate to the financial interests of the specific alcohol company's shareholders.

Pubs and Bars

Pubs and bars are designed to make drinking alcohol as convenient and comfortable as possible. Bars are also designed to make you forget about the outside world and to influence your mood. By influencing your mood, it becomes easier to influence your behavior. Most bars have curtained or frosted windows so you can't even see ordinary life slipping by. The overall aim of any bar is to get you in, keep you in, and kick you out when the barman decides that you have had enough to drink. Once you've drank too much, you become a liability. It's much better for the pub owner to kick you out on the street after you have had too much to drink where you become someone else's problem.

Alcohol Propaganda

Alcohol advertising is everywhere. It's designed with one purpose in mind, to make you want to buy and drink more alcohol. Often, alcohol marketing is associated with images of bravado, sex, cleverness, or social acceptance.

One core message which is constantly being declared by these clever alcohol propaganda campaigns is that drinking alcohol is harmless once you drink responsibly. Another is that alcohol use can be beneficial to your health.

The industry sees itself as being at the forefront of promoting responsibility, but that responsibility is ultimately placed on you, as the consumer, not Big Alcohol, as the producer. In almost any other industry, if a consumer gets injured or dies because he has used a product, the company that has made the product is at least partially liable.

Not with BA.

At least not yet!

The health producing elements of BA marketing are just as dubious. I will examine this a bit more later in the book.

Persistent Presence

Once you stop using this drug, the alcohol industry is not going to hold up the white flag, pack up, and leave you alone. Alcohol and alcohol propaganda are everywhere, you cannot avoid it.

As you walk your dog in the morning, you are still going see the massive billboard whose only function is to entice you to drink the best lager in the world.

As you sit down in the evening, watching your favorite soap opera, you will still see ads for whiskey, vodka, gin, and wine, all trying to fill your head with images of beauty, fun, and the carefree drinking life.

For the foreseeable future, as you push your shopping cart through your local supermarket, the alcohol will remain on sale, the bottles of booze are going to seem like they are in everyone else's trolley, and you'll still hear the tempting announcements shouted over the public address system.

It may seem like only you are the odd one out. You may view alcohol as the forbidden fruit and feel like you are the only one in the whole world who can't take advantage of it. This is just a part of the propaganda. We all want to fit in, after all. It's this need for social acceptance that can make quitting alcohol seem extra difficult.

To even things out a bit, let's peel back some of the layers of bullshit.

Scraping Off the Bullshit

The value we can get through understanding this disinformation cannot be stressed enough. We have been brainwashed by this propaganda throughout our lives. The source of that brainwashing is not going to disappear. There is nothing you can do about it! What you can do is adjust your thinking so that the alcohol propaganda has no effect on you.

Alcohol is a permanent fixture in our culture. You need to change the way you think about alcohol to give yourself the best chance of success.

You have to help yourself.

You need to take total responsibility for all your actions. Because you now understand the nature of the propaganda, and how deadly alcohol actually is, you are already more educated about this drug than most other people. You understand that alcohol is not the harmless drink that it is portrayed to be. You know from first-hand experience the damage that using alcohol as a tool has caused in *your* life. You have been at the receiving end of this bullshit for far too long!

*Members of the *Independent Scientific Committee on Drugs*, including two invited specialists, met in a 1-day interactive workshop to score 20 drugs on 16 criteria: nine related to the harms that a drug produces in the individual and seven to the harms to others. Drugs were scored out of 100 points, and the criteria were weighted to indicate their relative importance. Heroin scored 55 out of 100. Alcohol scored 72 out of 100. You can find more information from some of the contributors here: www.sg.unimaas.nl/_OLD/oudelezingen/dddsd.pdf

The Alcohol is not to Blame

"The best years of your life are the ones in which you decide your problems are your own. You do not blame them on your mother, the ecology, or the president. You realize that you control your own destiny."
Albert Ellis

The Alcohol Tool

It is true, once alcohol is inside your body, it can cause a lot of damage and many health issues. Among other things, it can cause of a swollen liver, a saggy heart, and a pickled brain. The key element to understand here is that alcohol needs to be on the inside of your body before it can cause any of these things to happen. Alcohol can have no effect on you from the outside.

Blaming alcohol for your bad health, your bad behavior, or your bad life is just a cop out. Alcohol is a means to an end. We use it as a tool to shift ourselves from emotion A to emotion B. We use alcohol to shift our feelings from being bored to being interested, from being sad to being happy, or from worried to not really caring about anything at all! The point is, we always have a reason to drink, even if that reason is to get blind drunk so you don't have to think about your problems any more.

Our Reasons to Drink

Think about way back when you first started drinking alcohol. Even then there was a reason. Nobody starts drinking alcohol because they like the taste. If it were the taste that attracted us to drinking, our younger selves would have no problems with drinking hard liquor. In fact, when you first start drinking, the more alcohol contained in a drink, the less you will like the taste.

Drinking pure alcohol, or ethanol, is not only unpalatable, it could also prove deadly. It won't take much pure alcohol to raise your blood alcohol content to dangerous levels.

When we first start drinking, it's more likely the non-alcoholic components of the drink that we like the taste of. We like the taste of the mixer, the fruit juice, or the high fructose corn syrup that sweetens the drink and makes it more palatable. The alcohol industry knows every trick in the book to create the type of alcohol that powers your taste buds.

As I have already said, the biggest reason for our personal alcohol use is because we are raised in a culture that uses alcohol. We are trained through imitation, mimicking our elders and peers. If a child is raised among adults who regularly drink alcohol, guess what they will want to do when they grow up?

By the time we are old enough to legally drink alcohol, alcohol consumption is not seen as a drug, or dangerous, it is just seen as another normal thing we do.

Then we pass the habit down through the generations. I remember very well the day my father bought me my first pint. I then passed on this wonderful tradition by being the one to buy my son his first pint of beer. I actually took great pride in the act of sitting him down at my local bar, in front of all my friends, and buying him his first pint of Guinness, all the while beaming with satisfaction.

Selective Drug Encouragement

Of course, as a culture, we don't think the same way about all drugs.

Even though I smoked for years, I hated that my son took up the habit. The first time I saw him with a cigarette stuck out of his mouth, I was so disappointed and fearful. I knew he had been hooked into the image of a young-buck smoker. He held it in his mouth with a swagger that said - *I'm a tough guy*! I recognized the look from myself, all those years ago when I was his age, thinking I was the coolest dude on the planet with my filter tip hanging from my lips. I remember practicing the look in the mirror. And I knew that no matter what I said to my son, it wouldn't make a blind bit of difference.

The point is, smoking is a killer, everyone knows that. Smoking anything is not something we would encourage our worst enemies to do, least of all our own children.

If I thought my son was mixing with people who were taking heroin, I would do everything in my power to stop him from seeing them ever again, or them from being around him. But, in terms of overall harms, alcohol use is significantly worse than heroin use!

We send the message that heroin is a terrible and evil scourge on our society and that it must be stamped out at all costs. We impose massive punishments on anyone who is caught dealing in this and most other illegal substances. However, to blatantly encourage our youth to use alcohol is fine!

The Nature of Booze

In terms of our personal use, alcohol is merely a means to an end. Alcohol is our drug of choice. If we weren't using this drug, we would be taking some other drug. This is because it's not about the drug, it's about the end result.

Alcohol is an inert liquid. It's not capable of doing anything on its own. It cannot physically jump out of the bottle and into your mouth. It cannot psychically connect with your mind and force you to drink it. It cannot persuade you with emotional arguments, it cannot threaten you, nor can it plead or beg.

You must be a willing participant in placing yourself in harm's way. You have to deliberately raise the glass to your lips and pour the liquid into your mouth. Once the alcohol is in your mouth, you must swallow each mouthful. For alcohol to become a big problem in your life, you have to repeat this same simple process, sip after sip, again and again and again.

It's worth repeating here that quitting alcohol is very, very simple. You simply refuse to put another drop of alcohol contaminated liquid into your mouth. You don't buy it, you don't pour it, and you don't drink it.

If this is the only step you ever take, your alcohol problems will disappear for good.

How can you have a problem with alcohol if you don't drink it?

Stopping drinking the stuff is the first simple step. Next, you need to break apart the life that you've built around your drinking.

Alcohol's Healthy Benefits

"Advertising is legalized lying."
H. G. Wells

The Invisible Hand

As far back as I can remember, there has been a connection between health and consuming alcohol in moderation. Every so often, you will read an article which extolls the health benefits of drinking wine, beer, or whatever alcoholic drink happens to be in vogue at the time.

Once you start delving into some of these articles and stories, you will find that most of them are at best myths and at worst downright lies. Somewhere lurking in the background of the majority of these "health benefit" stories, is the invisible manipulating hand of an alcohol manufacturer.

Healthy Binge Drinking?

Even if all the alcohol benefit stories were true, they would not make a blind bit of difference to you and I. Why? Because any of the purported health benefits derived from drinking alcohol are always linked with moderate drinking, not daily binge drinking.

The reason we heavy drinkers convince ourselves that there are health benefits to drinking alcohol is because we really do not want to quit. We are way too cozy sitting in our comfort zones to want to break out and change our behavior. We like what we are doing, even though we might not like some of the consequences.

When we hear that there are health benefits to drinking wine or beer, we conveniently ignore the part about consuming alcohol in moderation. The alcohol marketers are well clued in to this type of selective inattention.

What is Safe Drinking?

Another issue is that nobody can agree on what counts as moderate drinking or how much alcohol consumption is considered to be safe. One group might say that on any one occasion, one unit of alcohol for women and two units for men is a moderate and safe level to drink. Another group will tell you that the safe limit is one *drink* for a woman and two *drinks* for a man. What is the difference between a unit and a drink?

There are different rules for how many units or drinks you can consume in a full week or if it is safe to drink every day. The difficulties of calculating how much you should be drinking are made more convoluted by taking into account your age, height, weight, what you have just eaten, your present health, your racial background, and so on.

Have you ever seen anyone taking out a pocket calculator and doing the math, right there at the bar, trying to figure out how much more they can safely drink? Have you ever heard anyone talking about stopping now because they have reached their unit limit? Alcohol reduces your inhibitions. Once you get that first drink into your body, it gets easier to accept the second, and the third, and so on. Once you have taken that first drink, what is the likelihood that you are going to think about alcohol units or drinking in moderation? Big Alcohol knows this only too well.

Moot Point

If you are drinking way too much alcohol, and if you have tried to moderate your drinking and failed, what difference does it make to you if there are health benefits to drinking small amounts? You do not drink small amounts! If you did, you would not be reading this book.

This is one of the lies that I told myself over and over again. I consistently convinced myself that wine was great for my health. All my knowledge was based on speculations that I had gathered over the years and twisted to fit my own logic. I never bothered to research any facts. For instance, I believed that red wine would thin my blood, which in turn would make it less likely that I would have a heart attack. I accepted that as a fact and used it as an excuse for my drinking. I imagined the wine coursing through my bloodstream, fighting the good fight and keeping my blood trim and in good shape.

I never bothered to look into any of these dubious claims for the simple reason that I did not want to be told any different. I never wanted to risk finding out the real truths. What if I stumbled across information that sparked small doubts in my mind. I just could not risk it! Don't get me wrong, it wasn't that I was making the conscious decision to lie to myself, I just accepted what I wanted to accept, end of story.

Looking For the Sticky Tape

The problem with delving into the facts of about your alcohol drinking is that you might not like what you find. The more you dig, the more chance you have of uncovering some piece of information that plants little seeds of doubt in your mind. We all know that these nasty little seeds can spoil our hooched-up fun. We don't want to spoil the party with the "truth", so we don't look. Ignorance is bliss!

Now that I've stopped drinking, I love having a dig around. When I see a study or a report about some crazy new benefit from drinking alcohol, I start looking for the strings, the tape, and the glue that holds these so-called facts together. And to be honest, they are never that hard to uncover.

The alcohol industry spends an awful lot of money in finding out why we do what we do. Many of the world's leading psychologists are taking home huge salaries and bonuses while working for the alcohol industry. Their job is to figure out exactly what makes drinkers tick. There is never any guess work in alcohol marketing and propaganda. The bottles are shaped in a way that will push your buttons, as are the labels, and the bar pumps. The whole experience, from the billboard advertising to the TV promotions and how the pubs are laid out, is solely designed to excite your emotions and get you to drink the advertised product.

To repeat, behind most "scientific" studies, reports, or findings, some of them from very well respected authorities and scientists, you will almost always find the hand and super large wallets of BA.

Protecting You from Yourself

At the end of the day, does any of this matter?

Alcohol is a poison! Alcohol is the end product of rotting fruit, vegetables, or grains. Look at the violent reaction the human body has when alcohol is consumed for the first time. Vomiting is a part of the body's defense system; your body will react in a similar fashion if you swallow *any* poison. It's only when you regularly persist in drinking alcohol that your body starts to develop a tolerance. This too is part of your defensive system. Alcohol tolerance does not measure how tough you are or how much alcohol you can handle. This tolerance process is a part of your immune system, it is a part of your body trying to protect you from yourself.

We kid ourselves into believing that drinking alcohol is something very natural. We tell ourselves that it's alright to use alcohol because humans been drinking it for thousands of years. If alcohol is so natural, why do our bodies always go through the same brutal reaction when we first drink it?
There are of course natural forms of alcohol intoxication. Very mild alcohol intoxication can happen if we eat over-ripe fruit. Alcohol production is also a natural part of your body's normal digestive processes. The reason your body is capable of dealing with these small amounts of alcohol is because we have evolved the ability over millions of years.

Furthermore, it is impossible to become addicted to the alcohol just by eating over-ripe fruit for a couple of reasons. Firstly, you would have to consume a huge amount to get a buzz. You would fill your stomach a long time before drunkenness could happen.

The second reason has to do with the seasonality of fruit. Fruit is only available for a couple of months of the year. Over-ripe fruit is only available for a few days max. It is difficult to habitualize something which only appears for such a short time frame.

Manufactured alcohol is certainly not natural. As we have seen, there is no shortage of alcohol to drink. Once you have the money, you can buy as much as you want. Drinking a lot of manufactured alcohol introduces alarming amounts of toxins into your body. This in turn causes your body to work very hard just to keep you alive. The more you drink, the harder your body has to work. But there are limits to how much your body can take.

Moderation: One Drink at a Time

"Complete abstinence is easier than perfect moderation."
Saint Augustine

Lifelong Restraint

Is alcohol the only drug where moderation is even suggested? Is it the only drug that has the "responsible use" label attached to its use?

If you told your doctor you were addicted to heroin, what would she say - *Moderation's the way to go? Just cut back on the amount you're injecting! You're not being a responsible heroin user.*

Moderation means restraint. It means holding yourself back, not letting yourself go to the level that you really want to go. Is that what you want? To be forever holding yourself back? Could you really live the rest of your life like that, forever denying yourself the whole reason for your drinking?

Drinking to Drunk

Is drug moderation even possible? Alcohol is a substance that reduces your competency. It also reduces your inhibitions. Once you start drinking, you will generally find it difficult to say no to a second round. Once you've had the second, you'll find it even more difficult to say no to the third. Once you have had the third ... well, you know where I am going with this. This is the life of a person who likes to drink until they get drunk.

Have you ever tried to moderate your drinking?

How successful were you?

Crash Moderation!

If you are anything like me, alcohol moderation probably looks something like this.

You stop drinking during the week. Perhaps you decide that from now on you are only going to drink on Tuesdays, Thursdays, Fridays, and Saturdays. You will not touch a drop for the other three days. Or maybe you choose to only drink over the weekend, on Friday, Saturday, and Sunday.

You manage to stick to your non-drinking days. It is difficult. As with any habit, when you are forcing yourself not to do something, you cannot help but think about it. Your "days off" act as a countdown to the weekend. You will tell yourself that the weekend will soon be here soon and that once Friday afternoon arrives you can let your hair down and enjoy yourself.

Friday finally arrives. You get on with whatever you have to do. All day long you anticipate the taste of your first drink. You are salivating once your deadline to drink arrives and you cannot wait to get to the pub, to the restaurant, or home to get that first sip.

You have sacrificed all week long and now it's time to get your well-deserved reward. You have denied yourself, proved that you are strong, and you don't feel the need to set any limits on how much you can have on your "drinking" days, you just go for it. Not drinking all week long was moderation enough. You congratulate yourself for a job well done. It's time for you to let your hair down and celebrate … you did it! You restrained yourself all week long! Yay!

Again, if you are like me, you have also tried moderating the amounts of alcohol you drink in any one session. You go to the bar with the intention of only having four drinks, instead of your usual ten. You say that you are only going to have two glasses of wine instead of normally polishing off the bottle. You have even succeeded a couple of times, which only goes to prove that you have no problem with alcohol, that you can take it or leave it.

Moderating your drinking once you have started drinking is way harder than taking a full day off. When you take a day off, for the most part you can put alcohol thoughts out of your mind as best you can and get on with your day. Once you have taken a drink, however, the urge to continue will always get stronger. You know that one drink will start the thoughts for another; this is basic alcoholic cause and effect. As you know, once you have one drink it is harder to say no to the second.

Moderation only makes sense in a world of moderation. We do not live in that world. We live in a world where excess is king.

Plus, have you ever heard the saying *absence makes the heart grow fonder*?

Forever Moderating

Let's take a look at moderation from a realistic point of view. Moderation is always open ended. What I mean by that is that moderation is something you will have to do for the rest of your life. You cannot moderate for a week and then move on. You have to moderate day in and day out, every week, every month, and every year.

Are you up for that?

Is that something you want?

Do you have the self-control, the mental balance, or the patience to continue to moderate forever?

Do you have the lifelong strength to moderate when all you really want to do is get drunk?
How is that easier than just removing alcohol from the equation, from your life?

Stopping drinking is a task you only have to complete once. You stop and that is it! So long as you don't restart, you are done!

Using to Abusing

My alcohol-drinking life has always been about drink to get drunk, use to abuse. I have tried moderation and I was miserable for most of the time. I would always last a couple of weeks, then I'd simply go back to my normal drinking patterns with no fuss. I would just go right back to drinking whatever and whenever I felt like it, pretending to myself that everything was alright.

Whenever I tried moderation, I did not drink any less alcohol overall. I just drank less, or none, during the week and way more at the weekends. Why? Because of scarcity. Starting from Friday evening, there was a time-limit on my drinking. I knew I would be right back on the moderation diet once Monday morning came. I knew I would not get the chance to "enjoy" myself for another five days, so I might as well enjoy myself right now. This is the same form of psychology at play when the barman shouts for last orders.

Tolerance Compared

I now know the true nature of alcohol and the negative effect it was having on me. Alcohol is a drug. The more you use this drug, the more your body fights against it by building an immunity to its intoxicating effects. The more immune you become, the more you have to consume to get the same buzz.

There are some drugs, like LSD, where the tolerance builds up very quickly. You can only take so much and that's it. It is pointless taking any more because you won't get high.

That's not the case with alcohol. The more tolerant your body becomes, the more alcohol you need, period. The more alcohol you need, the more you use, the more you use, the more you need. All the while, because tolerance does not mean protection, the toxic damage is accumulating.

Can I Moderate My Drinking?

When I was drinking alcohol, the desire to drink was insatiable. It was always there. Moderation was impossible for me because I just did not drink with moderation in mind. Once I couldn't drink alcohol to get drunk, what was the point of drinking? Could I have learned to use alcohol in moderation? If I am being honest, I could have done it but I think it would have driven me mad.

We live in a world of manipulation and exploitation. Vast sums of money are spent every day researching and developing ways to control your mental wiring. There are people out there whose only job is finding out what makes you tick, then seeking out the methods to exploit your weak spots for profit. The best possible customer is an addicted customer. When you are an addicted customer, you are a slave to the product, whether that product happens to be alcohol, cigarettes, double whammy cheeseburgers, or your favorite brand of soft drink.

Do I think that I could moderate my drinking into the future? Yes, if I tried hard enough. But why would I want to put myself through that kind of hell? I don't see any personal gain in being smashed out of my head anymore and I have no desire to drink just for the taste, there are plenty of tastier things out there.

Big Alcohol has permanently lost its hold over me.

Brainwashed Since Birth

"Emancipate yourselves from mental slavery. None but ourselves can free our minds."
Bob Marley

Preaching to the Choir

Moderation is also a great brainwashing tactic. It keeps us firmly entwined in the alcohol loop. By thinking that we can moderate our drinking, we continue to perceive alcohol as a benign substance. It is classified as a beverage, not a drug, after all. If you have tried to moderate in the past, you know that once you have taken your first drink, it's too late. The alcohol can only influence you from the inside. You have opened the door, let the flow begin, and the alcohol can get on with its effect. Alcohol is a diuretic, so it makes you a little thirsty. Under the influence, you get a bit more relaxed and you're less likely to make the right choice, to say no! It's so easy to say - *I'll just have the one more.*

Heavy drinkers or alcoholics, whatever you want to call them, are the bread and butter of the alcohol industry. BA doesn't need to waste propaganda time or dollars on the heavy drinker. Heavy drinkers are self-propagandized enough. They are already slaves. When you are a heavy drinker, the only decision you will make is what brand of alcohol to drink. And even then, once you get set in your ways, there is no decision left to make. Sooner or later, we all find our default brand.

I was a Guinness man. No other brand would do. Not Beamish, nor Murphy's, not even O'Hara's. Why? I don't know why! Because that is the brand I always drank. Because that was the brand I most identified with. Because I liked the Guinness advertisements better than the Murphy's. Because Guinness has been around since 1759. Because Guinness had done a much better job of enslaving me than any of the other brands. Because I liked the way they could draw a shamrock onto the head. I don't know why! I only know that it only felt right when I was drinking Guinness. That is what brand marketing is aimed at, it just feels right when you make your purchase.

Marketing the Youth

Big Alcohol, like Big Tobacco, concentrates most of their marketing money on building for the future. They aim most of their propaganda ammunition at young people who are just starting out in life, those who haven't yet become tied to a particular brand. The industry freely admits this. You will rarely see any of their propaganda messages aimed at old farts sitting on bar stools in the local pub. Every advert depicts youth, strength, vitality, daring, sex, good looks, and so on. Then these depictions are associated with the alcoholic product. It's all basic Pavlovian conditioning.

Young Lads on the Piss

Let's take an example of a typical group of young men having a night on the town. At the most extreme level of the moderation scale, a male is allowed 14 alcoholic drinks in a week, with no one day exceeding 4 drinks. This is not taking into account how many units of alcohol are in the drink or any other significant factors.

Among our group of lads, there is one guy who is on the local soccer team and he is trying to keep his alcohol drinking in check. He does not want to go above the four drinks on one night rule. They go from one pub to the next, buying in rounds. It doesn't take very long before our young soccer player reaches his self-set limit and makes the decision to stop. Now he has a choice. He either leaves the bar and goes home or he sticks around but only has soft drinks for the remainder of the night.

Because he has already consumed four pints, his aggression levels might already be slightly raised and his inhibitions will definitely be lowered. His companions continue to knock back the pints and are now in the mood for joking around and giving our moderation lad a hard time. He feels like drinking more, just to shut them up.

He ignores all the remarks, however, and soldiers on. By the end of the night he has become very sober. His mates, on the other hand, are completely drunk, shouting and balling, and carrying on in general. Now, he is wishing he had not stuck around after all.

How many times will he tolerate this same situation? Most young men will not even get to that first soft drink. As soon as the teasing starts, they will either continue drinking alcohol or they will leave.

Early Influencer's

The brainwashing starts early and carries on throughout your life. It comes at you from all angles. Your first brainwashers were most likely your parents and their friends. Then you had normal alcohol use portrayed in television programs and advertising slots. There were the billboard posters that you saw on your way home from school, all depicting various happy situations where alcohol was involved. Maybe even your teachers had an influence. If you went to church you might have seen alcohol as part of the service.

Alcohol is used at most celebrations, at parties and birthdays, at Christmas and Easter, at graduations, christenings, weddings, and funerals.

You also play a big part in your own brainwashing, especially once you start drinking. You develop certain alcohol rituals over the years. You get used to drinking in a certain way - you like to drink from a particular type of glass, for instance. As we have seen, you will habituate to a favorite beer, a way of drinking that beer, and most of your friends will tend to drink similar types of alcohol.

Chapter Three - The Language of Addiction

"Victorious warriors win first and then go to war, while defeated warriors go to war first and then seek to win"
Sun Tzu, The Art of War

Extracting Meaning

Think about our language like a massive box of tools. Each word within that language is a separate tool. Imagine the sorts of tools you would find in a toolbox in your home, a hammer, a chisel, a saw, a file, a bottle of glue, a paint brush, or a nail. Each of these tools has a different function. The same with each word or sentence in your language toolbox. We use our language in an attempt to comprehend and make sense of what's going on in the "outside" world and to communicate what's happening in our "inside" world.

Just as you can use a hammer for many types of jobs, most words in our language have several different meanings. For instance, according to the website dictionary.com, there are 26 meanings for the word *dog*.

Your idea of a dog might be completely different to mine, but in general we can agree that a dog is a four legged animal that barks and wags its tail. It could be a big dog like a Great Dane, or a small dog like a Pekingese. They are both dogs, in the general sense of the word, but they are really quite different. There are hairy dogs and bald dogs. There are dogs that have deep bass barks and others that have high squeaky, persistent, and very annoying barks.

The same sort of logic applies to any physical object. If you can physically touch something, you should be able to describe it so that the person you are trying to communicate with understands what you're on about. As another example, if I say the word chair, you understand immediately that what I am talking about is something you can sit on to eat a meal or stand on to change a light bulb. The same applies to every noun such as door, apple, gate, computer, pen, weasel, and so forth.

If you don't speak English, however, and I try to describe an apple to you, I'll have some difficulty getting my meaning across. I could say the word apple, over and over all day long, and you won't understand what the hell I'm saying. I could try to mime out the shape of an apple, mimic an apple falling from a tree, or I could pretend I was eating an apple, and so on. You may or may not understand. If I pull an apple from my pocket and hold it up in front of your face, you will immediately get it. Even if you have never seen an apple before, you should understand that what I am showing you is a type of fruit, or at the very least a type of food.

So, when I'm trying to describe a physical object to you, I can overcome the language barrier by showing you the object or a basic representation of that object, such as a photo or a model. But how do we communicate when there is no physical object, no photo, and no model? What happens if what I am trying to describe to you is only an abstract concept or an idea? How do I communicate my meaning then?

Tools or Weapons

Let's take a couple of examples, the words love, hate, jealousy, or emotion. You can try to describe the idea of what any of these words mean to you, an interpretation or a specific manifestation of them in your life, but you cannot show anything concrete in physical reality. That is because these abstract words have no specific physical object. I cannot just pull some hate or love out of my pocket and hold it up for you to examine. Even though I can write the words love and hate, they are only representations for something that has no material basis. There is nothing that you can point to and say *this is love* or *there is some hate*. These words are general concepts that mean something different to everyone.

Let's take a closer look at the word *love*. What is love? Can you point to anything and say *this is love*? If you had to describe love to someone, how would you do it? One of the ways we can try to communicate *love* is in terms of a physical reaction - *I feel butterflies in my stomach when I think of you* or *my heart flutters when you're near*. We can also try to represent love through symbolism. I can show you a solid object like a heart, red roses, or even a well-worn and treasured photograph, explaining you that these objects represent how I feel about love. We can talk about happiness, caring, passion, or forever. But none of these explanations make the true concept of love any clearer. All we are doing here is using one abstraction to describe another.

When you try to communicate your understanding of the word love, there are certain aspects of your depiction that will be understood by all; then there are certain aspects that will be understood by only some people, probably those closest to you. Finally, there will be aspects of how you perceive love that nobody else will understand. This is the same with all abstracts. Beauty is in the eye of the beholder. So is anger. So is jealousy. So is problem, solution, good, bad, or deviant.

So is the abstract of alcoholic! That's what we'll look at in the next section.

Are You Alcoholic?

"Words are, of course, the most powerful drug used by mankind."
Rudyard Kipling

The Perception of Alcoholic

Alcoholic is a word which has many meanings, depending on who is using it. For instance, a doctor may use it to define a condition or a disease. A judge might use it to ascertain culpability in a crime. A job interviewer might hear the word and see it as trouble in the making, while a member of Alcoholics Anonymous might see it as a permanent illness and disability.

Alcoholic is a word that nobody wants to be personally associated with. It is a word that prevents many heavy drinkers from even admitting to themselves that they might be in trouble. In perception, there is a fine line between problem drinker and alcoholic!

What are the common perceptions of alcoholic and alcoholism?

Alcoholism is commonly perceived as bad. To be an alcoholic is a label that can stick with you for the rest of your life. Once you are known as an alcoholic, you will be perceived as weak, troubled, pathetic, or out of control, a lesser person who is not capable of handling their drink.

The alcohol industry reinforces this false perception by promoting its own abstract concepts of 'responsibility' and 'safe' levels of consumption. At the same time, Big Alcohol spends hundreds of billions of dollars connecting alcohol, and alcohol consumption, to the good life, to strength and virility, to sex appeal and passion. The goal of BA is to increase consumption and profits, maintain and grow brand loyalty, while at the same time distancing itself and its products from any negative consequences that result from its use. Very responsible!

Should You Call Yourself an Alcoholic?

How does this all play out in relation to you and stopping drinking?

The words you choose to use are powerful tools that will help you to achieve your goals in this life. However your words, along with your thoughts and self-talk, can also be used as weapons against yourself.

If you want to apply the word alcoholic to yourself, only ever use it before you quit drinking. Never use the word to describe yourself once you no longer drink alcohol. This word carries too much emotional baggage for you to be hauling it around for the rest of your life. Think about it, calling yourself an alcoholic after you have quit does not make any sense. How can you be an alcoholic if you don't use alcohol?

When I stopped using alcohol, I stopped being an alcoholic, full stop. When I quit smoking, I stopped being a smoker, and I stopped calling myself a smoker. Before I stopped drinking, I was technically classed as obese. In the last year, I've lost over 60 pounds. Do I continue to call myself overweight or obese? No bloody way! That would be completely idiotic and ridiculous. It's just as ridiculous to call yourself an alcoholic after you have stopped using alcohol, you are using the word as a weapon against yourself.

As the old saying goes, you are what you think you are!

I feel really sorry for people who have eliminated alcohol from their lives and yet still continue to use the alcoholic label against themselves. I once had a chat with a woman who hadn't touched a drop of alcohol in over 20 years, not a single drop! Yet here she was in front of me still calling herself an alcoholic and insisting that one drink would send her straight back to the beginning again. How sad is that!

Defining Alcoholic

Let's take a closer look at the word alcoholic.*

An <u>alcoholic</u> is a person *"suffering from alcoholism."*

<u>Alcoholism</u> is *"a chronic disorder characterized by dependence on alcohol, repeated excessive use of alcoholic beverages, the development of withdrawal symptoms on reducing or ceasing intake, morbidity that may include cirrhosis of the liver, and decreased ability to function socially and vocationally."* [Emphasis mine]

Let's break this definition down.

The first part of the definition that alcoholism is *"a chronic disorder".* Most of the drinkers I know, drink chronically. They never drink alcohol once and forget about it. Those who only drink once are known as non-drinkers. Alcohol drinkers tend to repeatedly use alcohol on a regular basis. And when alcohol gets into the human body, it causes dis-order. Like any other toxin, alcohol is a foreign substance that sets all your security alarm bells ringing.

The next part states that alcoholism is *"characterized by dependence on alcohol".* Dependence is defined as *"the state of relying on or needing someone or something for aid, support, or the like."* Most drinkers use alcohol as a way of relaxing, socializing, partying, etc, and would feel very uncomfortable, to say the least, if they could not drink at these times, even though most would never admit it. This sounds like dependence to me!

Which leads us to the *"repeated excessive use of alcoholic beverages".* Many of those people who drink chronically, and are dependent on alcohol, repeatedly exceed the recommended daily or weekly usage guidelines. They chronically drink more than two drinks for a man and one drink for a woman, or repeatedly use alcoholic beverages to excess.

Then we come to *"the development of withdrawal symptoms on reducing or ceasing intake".* How many drinkers to you know who suffer from withdrawal symptoms if they reduce or cease their intake? Many people have some difficulty sleeping if they don't have that alcoholic nightcap. Some feel mildly anxious at times when they would otherwise be drinking, and some may even feel slightly nauseous or sweaty. These are all symptoms of alcohol withdrawal syndrome. They are also symptoms of any hangover! This is the reason we call them hangovers. We never want to call them what they really are, critical signs of alcohol withdrawal. You reduce or cease your intake of alcohol when you go to bed drunk, you wake up with the development of withdrawal symptoms.

And then there is the final part of the definition, that alcoholism is characterized by *"morbidity that may include cirrhosis of the liver, and decreased ability to function socially and vocationally."* It is estimated that absenteeism and below standard job performance which is caused through alcohol use, and more specifically through hangover, costs an average of $2000 per year for every working man and woman in the United States. That adds up to a whopping total of $48 billion every single year. I think this could easily be described as a decreased ability to function.**

The same report, from the Annals of Internal Medicine**, concludes that a hangover "has substantial morbidity and societal cost". The article goes on to say, "Recent studies suggest that the alcohol hangover induces cardiovascular and psychomotor morbidity independent of the quantity of alcohol consumed or the frequency of ingestion"

There are many derivatives from the word alcoholic, like shopaholic, golfaholic, chocaholic, sugarholic, and foodaholic. Each of these refers to a habit. They refer to people who shop a lot, play too much golf, eat too much chocolate, sugar, or food. I've even heard of a curryholic who's wife divorced him because of his curry addiction! All jokes aside, none of these derivatives has the same negative undertone that is attached to the word alcoholic.

Recognizing You Have a Problem

I am not trying to lessen the seriousness of being an alcoholic or having difficulties in your life because of your alcohol drinking. This is a very serious situation to be in. However, if you look at this definition of an alcoholic, it can be applied a huge number of so-called 'normal' drinkers, not just those who realize that they have a problem. In other words, you are not in the minority. You *are* in the minority in that you recognize alcohol for what it is, an incredibly harmful and dangerous drug. You *are* in the minority in that you recognize the propaganda of alcohol marketing and how it tries to influence you, your life, and everyone around you - including your children. You *are* in the minority once you make the choice to do something about your drinking.

Recognizing that you have a problem is the first step towards change. Once you comprehend that there is a problem, you cannot return to incomprehension.

Normal vs Abnormal

When I informed my son that I was thinking of stopping using alcohol, I told him that I thought I was an alcoholic. I told him I felt that alcohol was preventing me from doing so many things in my life. He was absolutely shocked. He was shocked that I could use *that* word on myself. No way was I an alcoholic! He said I just needed to cut down on my drinking. Even though he knew how much I drank, he didn't think about it as anything abnormal.

Unlike most other drugs, using alcohol is mostly perceived as a normal part of our everyday lives. There are two ways for your drinking to be classed as abnormal. The first is when it is completely obvious that you have a big problem. Your drinking has increased to such a level that it is interfering with your daily life, and everyone who knows you can see it. The second way is when you stop drinking or you tell people that you are thinking about stopping drinking. Ironic as this sounds, only when you tell people you are going to stop drinking, or you have stopped, will they assume you have a problem. I've lost count of the amount of times I've got that knowing look, *oh dear, you're an alcoholic*!

I think part of the reason for this is because when you 'quit' drinking, you are calling attention to the nature of the beast. By stopping drinking you are putting a spotlight onto a truth about alcohol that most people do not want to hear. You highlight the fact that alcohol is a drug and as a drug it can seriously damage your health, or worse. We will see later how many people die as a direct result of long term alcohol consumption.

Wobbling the Self-Concept

We all carry around a mental picture of who we are. This known as our self-concept. Your self-concept might be *I'm a straight-talking kind of bloke who likes crazy days at the beach. I love having a few beers and mucking around. I work and play hard!*

Or, *I'm a hometown girl and I'm not really interested in travel. I love meeting up with my girlfriends once a week, we drink a few glasses of wine, and have some fun.*

Our self-concepts are at the heart of how we perceive ourselves. Our self-concept tells us who we are, how much confidence we have, what we like and dislike, how we feel, and so on. We go through our lives trying to maintain a certain harmony within our self-concept. It is our most treasured and emotional possession.

When you tell someone that you're getting alcohol out of your life for good, you are putting a wobble into the other person's self-concept. By highlighting the nature of the drug, you force them to think about their own drinking. Even if they quickly push such silly thoughts out of their heads, the idea of alcoholism still threatens their self-concept. They never want to see *their* glass of wine or *their* bottle of beer as a drug. Nor do they ever want to see themselves as drug users.

The self-concept is so jealously protected and deeply ingrained that most people will try anything and go to any lengths to protect and preserve it.

Most people protect their self-image by moving the blame for your alcohol problems away from the alcohol and placing it entirely on your shoulders as the drinker. It cannot be the alcohol because they 'drink' alcohol without causing themselves any harm (none that they are aware of at least - what the eye doesn't see, the heart doesn't grieve over). They can 'control' their drinking, they can take it or leave it. When they get drunk, they are only doing it because they want to, not because they are drinking to get drunk.

So they look at you and they think that you must have one of those addictive personalities, or you come from a family with addictive tendencies, or you were born with the 'addiction gene'. It cannot be the alcohol that has caused your problems, it must be you as a person. You are an alcoholic. And everyone knows that once an alcoholic, always an alcoholic.

Of course they feel sorry for you. But now everything is right with the world once again, the self-concept balance has been restored, and they can carry on their merry way believing what they want to believe.

Alcoholic Prejudice in Action

In my day job, I'm a writer of sorts. I write website articles for whoever will pay me the most money. I came across a job posting in February 2014, for a brand new website looking for long term writers. The commission was really good and most of the articles were about self-help and pop-psychology, the *how-to* type article. It seemed like a good opportunity for me, so I applied.

At the time, it was over a year since I had quit alcohol. I had built the website, alcoholmastery.com, from scratch and it was really starting to take off and help people. I was spending a lot of time making new videos and writing about how my life had changed for the better since I stopped drinking. I was really enjoying building the site but it wasn't paying the bills.

A couple of days after I submitted the application, I received an email asking if I would do a Skype interview. Great! I sent the guy some examples of my article writing, told him about the website and some of my plans for the future.

The day of the interview came around and everything was going fine. He wanted to know all about my style of writing, how long I had been writing, what my favorite genres were… all the typical interview questions.

He said he'd taken a look at Alcohol Mastery and although the videos could do with some work (which I knew), he thought the content was excellent.

Then, it got a bit weird because he started asking me about my alcoholism.

What alcoholism? I said.

He said *Well, you run a site about your drinking problems...*

I told him *I run a site about alcohol problems in general and some of the content is about the drinking problems I used to have, the ones I don't have any more since I stopped using alcohol!*

He said *he didn't want alcohol to get in the way of my work.*

I told him again that *I didn't drink alcohol so how could it ever get in the way of my work.* I said *alcohol used to influence and interfere with my work when I was drinking. But if I was being interviewed during those times, he would never have known that I had any problems because I wouldn't have told him!*

I knew where he was going with his *logic.* It was the typical - once an alcoholic, always an alcoholic line of thinking. When you stop using alcohol, you are automatically seen to have a problem! I couldn't argue with it. I did not want to argue with it. I knew the job was gone but I didn't really want to work for the guy anyhow. I stuck through the rest of the interview and closed the connection feeling really pissed off. He sent me an email a couple of days later telling me they had opted to go for someone else. It didn't come as a massive shock!

Common Responses to Not Drinking

When I tell people that I don't drink, I usually get some fairly common responses. Some people immediately go on the defensive. They might defend their own drinking habits, explaining that they have their drinking completely under control. Or they tell me how much they like drinking and could never imagine being without it - *Sure, isn't life too short!*

Some look at me with pity. Others look at me with suspicion, especially if they are out to get drunk. I am the guy who is going to remember everything the next day! I completely understand where they are coming from, I was there myself for most of my adult drinking life.

Losing Control

Alcoholism is not a lifelong malady that you will never overcome. I believe that drinking too much does become a bad habit for millions of people across every walk of life. But just like any other bad habit, this loss of control does not happen overnight. The habit is a dynamic process that we have learned over many years.

After you've quit drinking alcohol, why would you still associate yourself with alcohol in any way, shape, or form? It just does not make any sense. Some people will say that even if you still think about drinking, you've still got a problem. We'll talk about this later in more detail. Suffice to say here that sometimes you just can't help thinking about drinking. What matters is how you react. The actions you take about the drinking thinking is what counts.

Alcoholic and alcoholism are just words, no more and no less. They are convenient labels that simply fail to define anything. Nobody can agree on what the word means, even from a medical point of view. But it does not matter because they are only words.

Your interpretation of your situation and how you apply those interpretations to your new life are what matters the most. I never call myself an alcoholic because it implies that alcohol still has an influence in my life. It doesn't. I do not accept that I have a gene that is responsible for my past drinking any more than I accept that my drinking arose from a disease or that it has become a disease. If I accept any of those things, I lose much of my control.

To change anything first requires that you believe *that* change is possible. Next you have to believe that you can make *that* change.

Calling yourself an alcoholic, believing that you have a disease which forces you to drink alcohol, or that some sort of genetic malfunction is responsible for your *affliction*, locks you out of control. Maintaining the victim mentality of alcoholism, disease, and genetic abnormality, means you can never be in control. You will always be a casualty. The answers will always be beyond your ability. No amount of discipline, self-control, or self-awareness will ever make a difference to you. It's very difficult to beat self-inflicted inevitabilities.

Fortunately, change happens anyway. Change is one of the few things in life that is inevitable. You just need to be the one who is in charge. You need to be the one who's in total control over which direction that change is going to take.

* The source for the definitions is dictionary.com.
** http://annals.org/article.aspx?articleid=713513

Your Recovery

"Healing is a matter of time, but it is sometimes also a matter of opportunity."
Hippocrates

Dynamic Recovery

Recovery is another label that has become synonymous with addiction. As I said in an earlier section, recovery is also an abstraction. It is usually referred to as the place you will end up when you stop drinking... *'in recovery'*. The problem is that many people see themselves as being *'in recovery'* for the rest of their lives. They often call themselves *'recovering alcoholics'*, or a *'recovering addicts'*.

Recovery is a dynamic process with a beginning, a middle, and an end. No two people will go through the same experience. For instance, you may need more physical recovery than psychological recovery. Perhaps you've been drinking for a long time and your internal organs need a lot of restoration. In a nutshell, the recovery process will be:

1. You stop drinking alcohol.
2. Your body and mind go through the dynamic process of recovery.
3. You are recovered.

Recovery is about change. Recovery is never static. It is all about the process of transforming you from an alcohol user into a non-alcohol user. Just as said about the word alcoholic in an earlier section, you can never touch recovery. Nor can you taste it, smell it, hear it, or feel it. It does not exist as a thing. Again, it is a ongoing process with a beginning, a middle, and an end.

Sometimes recovery is seen as a process of restoration. It often implies a reversion back to a previous state, reverting to something or someone you used to be. I drank for the best part of my life and I know it would be impossible to go back to who I was before. Besides which I would never want to go back to that person. I am quite happy moving forward and getting as far away from that person as I can. It was my naiveté and inexperience which led me to use alcohol in the first place. I can never go back there. I want to learn the lessons that I should have learned all those years ago when I was too busy getting wasted. I also want to do the things that I have missed out on because of my past choices. Now I can look forward to each new day and everything that my new life has in store for me.

We'll look at the recovery process in a bit more detail later in this book.

The Symptoms and Side Effects of Quitting Drinking

"The language we use to communicate with one another is like a knife. In the hands of a careful and skilled surgeon, a knife can work to do great good. But in the hands of a careless or ignorant person, a knife can cause great harm. Exactly as it is with our words."
Unknown

Side Effects

Two other words to be cautious about using on yourself are symptoms and side effects. These words feature heavily in addiction literature. When we think about quitting, we often think about the symptoms and side effects that we might experience as part of the process. But are they the right words to use?

First, let's take a look at side effects.

Side effects refer to the unexpected results you may experience from taking an action. Let's take the example of using prescription pills for a problem you have with sleeping.

You visit your doctor because you're having difficulty sleeping. Your doctor examines you, asks you some questions, and then prescribes some sleeping pills. You take a pill an hour before you hit the sack and have no trouble getting to sleep. When you wake next morning, you have a headache and feel constipated. These are some of the side effects from taking that particular sleeping pill. Most medications have side effects. This is a result of the complex nature of our bodies, our internal chemical balances, and how everything you consume affects those balances in one form or another.

Symptoms

What about the word symptoms?

A symptom is a *"phenomenon that arises from and accompanies a particular disease or disorder and serves as an indication of it."*

Can *stopping* doing something really be classed as a disease? What about a disorder?

What do you imagine when you think about these words?

When you stop drinking alcohol, for a while you'll be completely out of your comfort zone. You're not used to doing without your crutch so you will feel temporarily dis-eased and dis-ordered! In other words, the ease and order that you've been used to in your life has been interrupted

However, we usually interpret the words disease and disorder as being something to fear. These words generally equate to feeling mental or physical suffering, to hospitals, injections, medications, relapses, and so on.

Searching for Answers

When you first start to think about quitting alcohol, you'll probably look for some helpful information. It's natural to want to know what to expect. Although we can't predict the future, we always like to have at least a rough idea of what might happen around the corner. An obvious place to start your search is the Internet - through Google, Yahoo, or one of the other search engines.

One of the problems with this type of search is the vast amount of information that is available.

For instance, the term *alcohol withdrawal* will present you with a sample of 3,220,000 pages. For *quit alcohol symptoms*, there are

8,350,000 pages. For *stop drinking alcohol*, there are 22 million pages.

Another problem is in the method by which this information is presented. The top results for each of the above keyword searches are either medical websites or media outlets. Each medical website uses the language of medicine. This can be quite challenging, even for the most fluent readers. The content of these sites can also scare you half to death. As for the media sites, let's just say you have to carefully dig around before you find an ounce of truth.

Money First

A third problem with some of the results that come up in these searches is that they tend to be very commercial. Google, and the other search engines, are businesses first and foremost. They exist to make money. Most of the top results in the search engines are advertisements. The companies and products you see have paid to be there.

The primary motivation behind any paid advertisement on the internet is to drive traffic back to websites. Often these websites offer expensive quit alcohol programs, hospital stays, or dry-out clinics. The profits of many of these companies rely on you believing that quitting alcohol is difficult. These websites, including some of the medical sites, are geared towards giving you the bad news about quitting drinking, emphasizing the bad symptoms and the terrible side effects, while minimizing any knowledge that focuses on your ability to quit on your own.

Some unscrupulous web sites will even go so far as to tell you that everyone who quits alcohol risks death from 'alcohol withdrawal syndrome'. I won't go into a lengthy explanation here about 'alcohol withdrawal syndrome', suffice to say that it covers every conceivable angle from losing a couple of nights sleep to death.

You Don't Need To Know Everything!

Even the best quality medical websites will emphasize the likely or possible symptoms and side effects that a person may experience while quitting.

Knowing this information is not in *your* best interests.

Think about it. Why are you trying to get alcohol out of your life? Is it because you're spending too much money on alcohol? Probably! But that's hardly the main reason. Are you just fed up with all the time you have been wasting while drinking? Again, possible, but not really the main reason.

Most people stop drinking alcohol because they are experiencing more pain than pleasure. What used to be an enjoyable pastime has become a life threatening addiction. The hangovers are getting worse. Dark thoughts about the future are becoming more commonplace. Someone close to you has probably expressed their concern, maybe even going so far as to tell you of their unwillingness to tolerate your drinking any further. All your fears about your future, your impending ill health, or your premature death are now causing you immediate and substantial fear and pain.

Once you feel enough pain, you will start to think about quitting. When you know that quitting is a real possibility, you can begin to look at your drinking, and everything that goes with it, in a different light. Maybe for the first time in your life, you'll understand just how destructive consuming alcohol really is. Now, every time you drink, there is no escape from the knowledge of that impending destruction. Each morning you wake with a horrible hangover, one that lingers for the rest of the day, you are taking one step closer to saying *enough is enough.*

Then, one day you decide to look for some information about quitting. If that information provokes fear about what might be in store once you do quit, you'll give yourself just enough of an excuse to have a rethink, maybe just enough to lose your resolve to quit.

To step over that starting line, you need as much encouragement as you can get.

The Demon Drink

"The supreme art of war is to subdue the enemy without fighting."
Sun Tzu, The Art of War

Conjuring Up Powerful Enemies

You often hear people talking about the "demon drink," like alcohol has a mind of its own, and an evil twisted mind at that.

Alcohol is only a liquid. It doesn't have a brain, so it can't think. Without your cooperation it can't make a sneak attack on your body, causing you to get drunk or give you a hangover. It cannot destroy your life or the lives of those around you once it remains in the bottle. You have to physically put each poisonous drop into your mouth and swallow, over and over, for alcohol to have any effect on you whatsoever.

You might think that calling alcohol *the demon drink* is only a joke, that these are merely words. But, behind these words are powerful thoughts and images. When you use terms like demon drink, evil alcohol, or the devil's brew, you increase the power that alcohol has over you.

Words like devil, demon, and evil conjure up images of fearful beasts, terrible acts of violence, cruelty, and destruction, as well as overwhelming power and influence.

The True Power of Alcohol

Why do we associate alcohol with these images? Alcohol is no more evil than water. As Sun Tzu says, when you go into battle, you should always try to weaken your enemy as much as possible. If you visualize alcohol as a substance with massive power, that's exactly what it will have over you, massive power.
This is the same principle that gives the one drink such great fear power. How many times have you heard an 'alcoholic' say, all it

takes is one drink to put them right back at the beginning. If that's the way you think, of course all it's going to take is the one drink. You need to treat alcohol for what it is, nothing but a nasty liquid.

My partner has a glass of wine every evening, often poured by me. From my perspective, the wine is nothing! It's a foul smelling, insipid, poisonous glass of rotting grape juice.

Seeing Past the Lies

The one glass and you're out theory is just that - a theory. It's not a reality until you make it a reality. If you believe it's true, *your thoughts* are what make it true, at least from your perspective. And that's all that really counts, *your* perspective. If you can see past the bullshit surrounding alcohol, why would you ever want to drink another drop, never mind a full glass? If someone tricked me into drinking a glass of beer, me thinking it was alcohol-free, would I be right back at the beginning. Like hell I would. I don't know what would happen next, but going back to my old self is certainly not one possibility.

So, always remember, alcohol has no power, unless you supply it!

You are much better served to think about alcohol in terms of how weak it is.

I used to visualize what was left of my alcohol habit as the Gollem from the Lord of the Rings. When I thought about my habit, I imagined a cowering, incompetent, sniveling, useless, impotent, and scared wretched creature who was slowly dying. This pathetic creature didn't represent the alcohol, but the part of me that still wanted to drink the alcohol. It portrayed the part of me that felt alcohol could still play a constructive role in my life. I took great pleasure in watching this bastard slowly die. Every time I thought about drinking, I would visualize the Gollem. Instead of being fearful about what was happening to me, I felt only happiness. Those images of my alcohol habit slowly dying only made me smile and gave me strength.

Power Yourself Up

Alcohol is always going to be a part of your life in one form or another. You can remove it from your immediate life, but not from your world. It's your choice how you think whenever you see other people drinking, when billboards and TV commercials try to fill your head with the desire to buy and consume, or when you pass the alcohol section in your local supermarket. Do you quickly look away, afraid of just looking at the rows of bottles? Or do you hold you head up high, puff out your chest, and be proud that all the alcohol propaganda just bounces off you? It's always just a trick of the mind. The choice is all yours!

Hitting Rock Bottom

"Rock bottom became the solid foundation on which I rebuilt my life."
J.K. Rowling

Where's Rock Bottom?

Do you need to reach rock bottom before you quit drinking?

What's your idea of rock bottom? Where is it for you?

Reaching rock bottom is associated with a place where a person may feel that they have nothing left to lose. It is where they have lost everything, their job, family, home, and so on. Rock bottom could mean that they don't have a roof over their head or enough food to keep their hunger at bay.

Every person's 'rock bottom' is going to be different, and this is another example of how damaging your language can be.

When I think of rock bottom, I imagine a person who is living on the street. They are hungry all the time, but they don't really care that, or about life or living any more. They have no ambition, no reasons for existing other than where they are going find their next drink, and they make no contribution to anything other than paying for the booze.

Rock bottom is the absolute pits, you can't go any further down.

In reality, you are nowhere near rock bottom until you're laying in a pine box which is being slowly lowered into a hole in the ground.

Listening and Seeing the Signs on Your Way Down

Most people who quit drinking alcohol, or stop using any drug, never hit rock bottom. Most people will realize what they are doing and try to get some help before they get anywhere close to the bottom.

There are plenty of signposts on the way down, all pointing to your need to change. If you honestly open your eyes and take a good look around, you'll have no trouble seeing yours.

The thing is not to wait until all your alternatives have dried up. Sooner or later the decision has to be made. And the sooner you can make that decision, the easier it will be to climb your way back up.

Are you going to allow your life to sink and keep sinking until the decision to do something is taken out of your hands?

Will you wait until change becomes an emergency, when a doctor says you must change or else?

Will you wait until your partner says they've had enough?

Will you not do anything until everything is gone?

Open your eyes and see the signs now, before it's too late.

There might be one event in a person's life that pushes them over the edge. Some people use that event as the springboard to change. For others it's still not enough. They need to go deeper.

Your personal rock bottom is where you choose it to be. All you have to do is to stop digging!

Chapter Four - Fears

"Fear keeps us focused on the past or worried about the future. If we can acknowledge our fear, we can realize that right now we are okay. Right now, today, we are still alive, and our bodies are working marvelously. Our eyes can still see the beautiful sky. Our ears can still hear the voices of our loved ones."
Thich Nhat Hanh

Searching For Answers

As I wrote about in an earlier chapter, many people start out on this journey with their fears all stoked up.

The desire to quit is there. They have had a moment of clarity, an understanding that things can't go on the way that they have been going, and they see a desperate need to make changes. They have tried moderation, without success. All it takes is a couple of slips and the old habits just come floating back to the surface.

This time, everything feels different. There's a determination that has been absent in all the previous attempts. Things need to be put right, and there is a resolve to persist with whatever it takes to beat this thing.

So they start searching for some answers. Their search might begin online. They talk to people in forums. They search the net looking for answers. They find blogs and medical websites. They look on Wikipedia, Yahoo answers, Quora, Facebook, Twitter, and so on. By the time they have finished, they are in more confusion than when they started. Instead of finding answers, all they have managed to do is further stoke their fears.

What Do We Fear?

Let me point out, once again, that quitting drinking is simple. Once you stop putting the alcohol into your mouth, you have achieved your initial goal. There is nothing more to quitting drinking than that. The rest is about adjusting to a new life and getting rid of the thoughts about alcohol. When you adjust to anything new, it takes time, patience, and a one-step-at-a-time approach.

Any fear you have is all in your head.

What do we fear most?

We fear the unknown. But every part of our future is unknown. Even with all the information and planning in the world, you never truly know what's going to happen until it happens.

We fear change. Our day to day lives are spent confined within our comfort zones. This is where we feel at our happiest and most content. Unfortunately, staying in your comfort zone means you won't change, at least not deliberately. Change happens all the time, most of it without our consideration. To change anything significantly in your life, you need to burst out of your comfort bubble.

Deliberately changing requires you to go through deliberate discomfort. The trouble is we don't like discomfort. In reality, getting out of your comfort zone doesn't take much change. You can make the adjustments little by little and still see some pretty significant results.

We fear failure. What happens if we go for it full on and we still fail? What if we tell everyone that we're quitting alcohol for good and we fail? What if we make a complete idiot out of ourselves? What if …?

We fear success. What if we successfully quit drinking? What will it be like if we can't have a drink EVER again? What will we do if we have a terrible day and want to commiserate with ourselves? What if we have a great day and want to celebrate with ourselves? What if …?

Affecting Fear

Fear can also be generated very easily through your environment. The people around you, those who are not too happy with your decision, can spark your anxiety and doubt about whether you're doing the right thing. They might figure that you quitting drinking makes them look bad. By calling attention to your own problems, you are also bring their drinking into the spotlight. They drink as much as you do, so if you have a problem with the amount of alcohol you were using, so must they! The fact that you are quitting will open a stream of thoughts for them that they would rather suppress.

Another thing that stokes fear is too much complication. Unnecessary complexity breeds doubt. Doubt breeds fear. The simpler you can make things, the better. The problem with simple is that it doesn't always mean easy. Most people are not looking for the simple way out, they're looking for the easy way out, the magic bullet. They want to make the decision, go to bed, and have the result magically appear in the morning, like a stocking full of Santa goodies hanging on the end of the bed.

Arriving in the Tomorrow

"Life is really simple, but we insist on making it complicated"
Confucius

There's a childish part in each of us that hopes for and pursues the most expedient possible way of doing things. We are always looking to get something for nothing. No hard work, no waiting long periods of time, we want what we want right here and right now. When you get something for nothing, there is almost always a price to be paid later. We've been doing this all along, taking the easy road out of our problems through drinking alcohol. The easy road means that we don't have to think too much about anything with a negative edge. Using alcohol is the one guaranteed way we have always found to stop the thoughts we don't want to think.

Now, we've finally arrived at the place where we have to pay the price for all that thought suppression. To climb out of this situation requires us to make a change in our thinking. We have to get away from putting pleasure first and offsetting the pain until tomorrow. We've already arrived in the tomorrow!

Deep down, we know that nothing worthwhile is easy to come by. Change is going to happen, whether we like it or not. We can make the changes ourselves, like quitting drinking, or we can allow those changes to just happen to us. It's our choice, either way!

Killing Your Determination

Your old fearful self will tell you that you are better off just staying the way you are. You will tell yourself that things are not all that bad. You will tell yourself that all you need to do is get your drinking under control and everything will be just fine. You are sure that things are going to be good because nothing bad will ever really happen to you.

Don't listen to that bullshit.

As humans, we're the worst predictors of our own future. We predict what we want to happen, not what is realistically going to happen. We predict the future using the thoughts and emotions that we're experiencing right now.

If you think about the future when you're in a bad mood or in the middle of a depressed moment, your future will almost always look negative. On the other hand, if you are in an extremely happy mood while you are imagining your future life, your outlook will be much more optimistic.

One of the big problems with fear is that it will kill your determination faster than anything else.

If you start to worry about things before they even happen, before you step over your starting line, there's always an easy fix waiting. All you have to do is go to the pub, to the store, fetch a few cans, or a bottle of your beloved booze, and all your doubts and troubles will be gone, however temporarily. You will be right back in your comfort zone - feeling good. What was it you were worrying about again? You are still going to stop drinking - just not right now. You'll just drink for a few more weeks. You will definitely quit in January. All the pressure of Christmas will be gone, and you are going to be much stronger. Tomorrow, tomorrow, tomorrow!

What Do You Want?

The way to avoid this type of fear is not to fill your head with all the bullshit in the first place. You need to get a grip on *your* reality. What is it you really want in your life? What is it that you're missing out on while you're stuck in the pub with all the other losers? Which of your dreams could you be getting one step closer to? Instead, you are sitting on your sofa drinking wine, filling some rich guy's bank account, sipping yourself away from your dreams while making his dreams come true!

I have also had to ask myself these questions. I had to try to be as honest with myself as I could. What happens when I quit? Will I still be able to mix it up with my drinking mates?

No!!!

Why not?

Because they're all losers who are doing the same loser bullshit that I've been doing for the past 30 years. That is the mentality that I had to use. My old drinking buddies were never going to change. And even if they did, I can't wait for that to happen, I just do not have the time. I have to look after myself and my family first.

Life is short, I need to start being a good dad and a good partner right now, I don't have the time to wait anymore. If I want to do quit drinking, it's got to be now. I don't have the time to pretend that everything is going to be alright. Everything is not going to be alright. If I continue to take this route through my life, everything is going to be far from alright. If I stay in the bar listening to these people, it won't be long before I'm being dragged back to where I was, back to the black.

Over the next few sections, I'll look at some of the most common fears.

Getting Over the Starting Line

The basic reality is always the same: the simplest part of quitting drinking is actually stopping doing it. You only need to do this once. You don't have to sweat about eliminating the alcohol from your body or repairing the damage that has been caused; your body will take care of that. You just have to stop putting the alcohol in.

The hardest part of quitting drinking is stepping over that starting line. Stepping over that line means you have to make the commitment to yourself and to the people in your life who you love, that you will never, ever drink alcohol again!

The most protracted part of quitting drinking is removing the alcohol thoughts. To remove any thoughts about alcohol is nearly impossible. You can't not suddenly not think about something that you've been doing for so long. Alcohol is going to pop up in your head every so often, as is drinking alcohol, getting pissed, and all the rest. Don't worry about it. There are plenty of ways for dealing with this. The greatest impact you will have on your future is not in eliminating the alcohol thoughts, but by changing *how* you think about alcohol and your relationship with it.

Taking Your First Step

The number one barrier that will stop you from making that commitment and actually taking that first step is your own fear.

It can take a big leap of faith to step over the starting line and often only a small crumb of fear to push you back across it again. So it's very important that you keep your fear exposure to an absolute minimum.

Fear of Death

"To fear death, gentlemen, is no other than to think oneself wise when one is not, to think one knows what one does not know. No one knows whether death may not be the greatest of all blessings for a man, yet men fear it as if they knew that it is the greatest of evils."
Socrates

One our greatest fears is the fear of dying. And a question that is asked by many who are about to set out on this journey is - can you really die from quitting drinking?

The hard truth is that some people do die when they suddenly stop drinking alcohol, there is just no getting away from that. I'm not a doctor, so I can't tell you what causes this. The one thing I do know is that, in those who have been drinking heavily for years, the vast majority of deaths are all related to the amounts of alcohol that have already been consumed, the damage that's already been done to the body, and the internal chemical imbalances that are constantly struggling to readjust.

What Is Your Risk?

The more alcohol you drink the more risk you face once you stop. If you don't drink every day, and on the days without drink you don't feel ill apart from your hangovers, you don't have much to worry about. That takes into account about 95% of all heavy drinkers.

If you use alcohol all day, every day, your chances of going through some severe withdrawal symptoms are a lot higher. Extremely heavy drinkers are at most risk. If you want information about just what types of withdrawal you might go through, there are plenty of websites where you'll find long lists of all of these symptoms.

I've tried very hard to come up with some reliable statistics about the numbers of people who die from quitting drinking every year. I find almost nothing. In any sane world, if a person dies once they have quit alcohol, the death would appear on the death certificate as death *caused* by alcohol consumption, not death caused by alcohol cessation. After all, the reason for the death is a failure of some part of the body as a direct result of drinking too much alcohol.

There is a mountain of statistics concerning the numbers of people who have died from *drinking* alcohol.

Fear Tactics

As we've seen, one fear tactic used by the *quit alcohol industry* is to say that no drinker should contemplate quitting on her own, without medical assistance. One reason they do this is play up the risks of death and severe withdrawal symptoms in an attempt to terrorize you into enrolling on one of their treatment programs. I'm not suggesting that the whole quit alcohol industry operates like this, but there is a certain cut-throat element within that industry and they're very vocal and well financed.

To put this into perspective, if you are at serious risk of death from quitting alcohol, there is absolutely no guarantee that medical attention can do anything for you. Take the case of Ryan Rogers. He was the subject of a documentary made by the National Geographic channel called *Drugged - High on Alcohol*. At the start of the film, we are introduced to Rogers and we see that he has a severe alcohol problem. At his worst, he was drinking 3 pints of vodka a day. He started drinking heavily when his father passed away four years prior to the making of the program. During the course of the film, he agreed to get medical help for his habit, however he died 17 days into this treatment. You can watch the documentary on YouTube.

I'm not suggesting that you shouldn't get help. People's lives are at stake. The threat comes mainly from the consumption of this drug, but in some cases the threat can come from the withdrawal. Lives can be saved with timely medical treatment, of that there is no doubt. Having said that, there is absolutely no need to mess your head up with thoughts about dying if you're not at risk of dying. If you are needlessly worrying about death, or any of the other severe symptoms that you might never go through, you might decide against taking that all-important first step in stopping your alcohol use. That would be the real tragedy!

Perspectives on Risk

Life by its very nature involves a lot of risks. There's a chance that you could die simply crossing the road or even walking down the street.

In August, 2012, Amanda Telfer, a London based human rights lawyer who was only in her early 40s, was killed as she innocently walked along a London street eating a banana.* An office building was being refurbished in Central London, which included replacing all the windows at ground level. New windows were delivered to the site and they were so heavy that they had to be lifted from the delivery truck using a heavy duty crane. One of these 13 foot windows was propped up against a wall when a freak gust of wind caught it and blew it over on top of the young woman. She died on the spot. She was just in the wrong place at the wrong time.

A few weeks ago, as I'm writing this, a young man was killed in our local theme park, Terra Mitica.** He was in Spain on holidays with his family and friends. Like many visitors to the area, the group took a day trip to this popular fun park. The young lad got onto one of the park's fastest rides, each circuit taking about 45 seconds and involving many high speed twists and turns. As the car he was sitting in spun into one of these turns, the security barrier which was supposed to hold him in the seat failed, snapping open and throwing him to his death.

The theme park has been operating for 14 years and it was the first time anything like this has happened. The chances of it ever happening again are infinitesimal, a few million to one. Even though I've been on that ride several times, I don't think I'll ever have the courage to get on it again. In fact, the same goes for any of the other rides. Why? Because I'm scared, I don't want to die just yet, thanks very much.

Is that logical thinking?

No, not at all! How many hundreds of thousands, if not millions, of people have gone through that park over its years of operation? How rigorously are these rides checked and rechecked? It's going to be a long time before anything like this happens again, if ever.

However, this is how the human brain works.

How many people go into hospital for routine operations and never come out again.

It happens all the time!

Some people have allergic reactions to medication, side effects that make them ill. Some of them even die. Does this mean that you should never go to hospital or take medication? Of course not!

There is an element of risk associated with almost everything in this life.

Quitting Vs Not Quitting

As I said earlier, there are no easily accessible statistics for problems with quitting drinking alcohol, but there is a mountain of stats for the problems associated with drinking alcohol.

Alcohol consumption is the cause of more than 200 different diseases and injuries. In 2012, 5.9% of total deaths were linked with alcohol use, about 3,300,000 people. Also in the same year, it was calculated that 139,000,000 net years of "healthy" life were lost (Disability Life-Adjusted Years - DALYs) because of alcohol use. Most worrying are the statistics for young men and women. 25% of all deaths for the 20 to 39 age group are alcohol related.

Those statistics are catastrophic, and they prove beyond all doubt that your death risks are far greater if you stay drinking!

Quitting Is about Learning

Quitting alcohol is a learning process as much as it's about beating a bad habit. You need to learn new ways of having fun and dealing with the pressures in your life. In some instances, you'll be relearning old skills. In other instances you will learn new skills, skills you didn't learn when you were younger because you were quite happy to take the instant gratification route that alcohol offers.

Learning to live your life without alcohol should be approached in a similar way as you would approach learning any other skill.

Learning about Dangers

For instance, let's say I wanted to learn how to swim. I am not very confident in or near the water because I'm not a very good swimmer. I can swim some lengths of the local pool, but despite living 50 meters from the Mediterranean Sea, I don't swim because I don't trust my abilities. I've listened to too many horror stories about undercurrents and the like, blown them all up into my own nightmare scenarios, and I've seen the movie *Jaws* - five times!

If I took swimming lessons, one of the first things I would expect to be taught would be how to stay afloat and keep calm. I would also expect lessons in correct breathing, how to build my overall strength, the different swimming strokes, and so on.

Imagine if I arrived on the first day, all ready to learn this new life saving skill, and the instructor asked me to join him by the poolside prior to my first lesson. He says that before we get started, we must go through some health and safety practicalities. So good so far. Then he explains that people can die and have died while learning how to swim. He says that more people die on their first and second swimming lessons than during any that follow. He then goes on to explain in great detail what dying by drowning looks and feels like. I would never get into the water.

What Do You Need To Know?

Why are we filling the already fearful heads of people who want to quit drinking with all the dreadful things that might never happen? There is absolutely no reason for it. Most people are not susceptible to any terrible side effects of quitting, so why tell them of the possibility? There will be people who will say that it's your right to know. Is it your right to know that you could be knocked down any time you cross the road? Or is it your right to know that the airplane you are just about to board could fall out of the sky and smash into a million pieces on the ground?

Why would you want to know these things?

What will be, will be.

Take the precautions.

Speak to your doctor.

But above all, make sure you step across that starting line full of confidence in your own ability to quit, the confidence that you can do it!

* http://www.bbc.com/news/uk-england-london-19488111
** http://www.independent.co.uk/news/world/europe/british-teenager-dies-after-falling-from-rollercoaster-at-the-terra-mitica-in-benidorm-9590682.html

Going to Your Doctor

"My doctor gave me two weeks to live. I hope they're in August."
Ronnie Shakes

Many people ask me if I went to see my doctor before I quit. In the interests of full disclosure, I have to say I didn't. For better or worse, I knew what I was letting myself in for and I didn't want to hand over 50 Euro so that my doctor could tell me what I already knew – that I needed to quit drinking. Also, I didn't want his advice about a support group I could attend or which pills I should consider taking if the symptoms got bad.

The decision was mine to make. It was my personal choice. I am not suggesting that you shouldn't get medical advice before you start on your own journey. My advice to you is at least have yourself checked out first. Better to be safe than sorry.

Proof I Wasn't Going to Die Just Yet

I had quit drinking for almost a year in 2008. I didn't go through any major discomfort, and I obviously didn't die from quitting. Between the time I started back drinking, in November 2008, and when I decided to quit again in 2012, I didn't drink every day.

It's not that I didn't want to drink every day. At the time, I still thought about myself as a drinker and drinking played big part of my life. However, I was a single dad and I had to work. I had to drive long distances, just to get to work, and I had already experienced what it was like to be prosecuted for driving under the influence.

I would often miss a day or two of drinking just to prove to myself that I could do it. On those missed days, I would generally feel good. I had very little discomfort apart from some persistent thoughts for alcohol. But my mind frequently went through a mental tug of war. There was one part of me that insisted there wasn't a problem in having a drink, and another insisting that it wasn't good to drink every day. It was like a relentless bitching session going on in my head.

What these days off gave was the assurance that I was not in any danger from quitting. I knew that once I did quit, any battles that I faced would be in my head. As I have said before, the majority of the risk involves continuing to use this drug, not stopping using it. I didn't need a doctor to tell me that home truth.

Drinking Risks vs Non-Drinking Risks

I worked in the forest industry for a long time. I used chainsaws, wood chippers, forwarders, harvesters, handsaws, sledgehammers, and so on. I was also in daily contact with falling trees, flying branches, and crazy squirrels. In all my time working in this risky environment, I never had an injury, apart from the odd finger cut while I was sharpening my saw.

Almost every injury that I have ever sustained in my adult life has happened when I was drinking alcohol or should I say while I was drunk. I broke my ankle twice jumping over fences while drunk. On both occasions I bent my foot in a way that no foot should be bent. I've slipped and fallen more times than I care to remember. I've come off bikes, fallen down hills, and stumbled headfirst into ditches.

I have suffered from stomach problems and ulcers because of my drinking. I've had kidney problems, liver problems, and too many hangovers to even count. Drinking alcohol also weakened my immune system, which left me open to all sorts of bugs, flus, and infections.

Are you thinking about how much injury alcohol has caused to you?

Alcohol Tolerance

The human body is capable of reducing some of the effects of alcohol by developing tolerances. However, drinking the stuff is no less dangerous in the end. In fact, tolerance – or your ability to hold your drink – only masks the damage.

Because you are physically able to drink greater quantities of alcohol without feeling the effects, you might surmise that your body is developing an immunity. This is not true!

The more alcohol you drink, the more alcohol is floating around your system. These larger amounts of alcohol cause greater damage. Tolerance doesn't prevent or reduce that damage. Tolerance only alters the quantity of alcohol it takes for you to get drunk, you need to drink more the more you drink. Just because you don't feel the effects doesn't mean the alcohol is not affecting you. The more you drink, the more you can tolerate, the more damage is being caused. The more you can tolerate, the more you need to drink, and the more damage is caused. It becomes a vicious circle.

Drunken Fools

Other dangers of alcohol use include putting yourself in compromising situations when you're drunk. Even if you're in the best of health and with all your wits about you, you need to be very careful about walking through most city streets late at night. How many times I have seen drunken young men picking fights with much larger opponents in the belief that they are invincible.

Don't be fooled into thinking that quitting drinking is going to be easy or without its own risks. However, the dangers involved in quitting drinking are minute compared to the dangers of continuing down the alcohol path.

Again, if you have any doubts, go see your doctor. You should aim at stepping over that starting line with as much confidence as possible. That means eliminating as much negative thinking as you can.

Your "Symptoms" After Quitting and Making Comparisons

"Confidence is preparation. Everything else is beyond your control."
Richard Kline

Quite often, there is a lot of fear associated with the symptoms and side effects that might happen to you when you stop drinking. This is just another irrational fear because you have no idea what is really going to happen once you step over the line.

It's difficult, if not impossible, to make predictions about your future. How can you ever know what is going to happen? Keep your future forecasting to a minimum, especially when it involves worrying about the negatives. You don't need to know most of the information about what might happen; most of it won't concern you. Reading or listening to the wrong type of negativity has a tendency to manufacture all sorts of negative thoughts in your mind! Sometimes, ignorance is bliss!

Keep It Simple!

You don't need to know every symptom, craving or side effect that could possibly affect you. This type of thinking is what author Wayne Dyer calls worrying about the *Wouldas, Couldas, Shouldas* of life. There can only be what *is*! Nothing more! Everything else is nonsense or speculation at best. Remember that what you think about most of the time will probably come to pass.

If you visit your doctor because you've got a pain in your belly, will she tell you about all the possible causes? Does she go through the full list of side effects of each medication she prescribes? Does she tell you every conceivable symptom that you should steel yourself against?

NO!

Why not?

To begin with, she doesn't have the time. Second, she knows that the more she tells you about these things, the more likely you are to experience the symptoms and side effects as a result. This is because your thoughts and emotions can easily affect you physically. Sometimes thinking about a "symptom" is all it takes to create the symptom. Every hypochondriac knows this.

Your doctor will tell you the bare minimum you need to know. Get lots of rest, take time off work, take these pills, and drink plenty of water. She will only explain the things that will benefit you.

Sticking to the Controllable

It's the same with quitting alcohol. Don't listen to or read up on every little thing that could go wrong or might go wrong. Stick to concentrating on the positives. Focus on those things that you can control, on the things that will help you in making your adjustments.

In my YouTube videos, I don't like talking about the symptoms or side effects that you may go through, because you probably won't go through them.

Que sera, sera! Whatever will be will be, the future's not ours to see, que sera, sera, what will be, will be.

You will know exactly what you are feeling when you feel it, not a moment sooner. So don't torture yourself unnecessarily in thinking about all the possibilities that will never happen.

I do love making videos about the mountains of shit that can happen to you if you don't quit. I love to talk about sagging heart muscles (as well as the more obvious sagging problems), scarred and necrotic livers, and wet brain – or Wernicke-Korsakoff syndrome – an often irreversible form of brain damage affecting memory, intelligence, and information processing.

I love talking about the worst visions I have had of my alcoholic future. How I used to visualize my son's face as he stood over my alcohol poisoned sick body.

I love talking about those things because there can be a positive purpose in explaining them. If I can get a person to think about the dangers that they are creating for their health, the tragedy of the relationships lost, or the selfish destruction of one human life, it might bring that person one step closer to crossing their own starting line and never looking back.

Comparing "Is" with "Might Be"

One of the things that might prevent you from crossing that starting line is your fear of what *might* happen. That fear could be about not having alcohol in your life any more, not having a crutch to fall back upon, or thoughts about the withdrawal process and how much pain you might go through.

A good idea is to make some comparisons between what *is* happening in your life right now and what *might* happen once you quit.

Examine the pain that you are in at the moment. What type of pain is causing you to think about quitting alcohol in the first place? Think about every area of your life that has been affected by your alcohol use. These thoughts will force you to confront the creeping destruction that trails along with you every time you have a bout of heavy drinking. For some of you, this might be the first time in your life that you have thought about these things. These are the thoughts that will drive you on, giving you the motivation to push through any tough moments in the days and weeks ahead.

Always Being the Drunk

For me, I couldn't face living the rest of my life being *the* drunk at every occasion. My past was full of pain about how I was acting in front of my son and the other members of my family. How could I feel pride in myself when I was contributing toward my son's alcohol habits? I have always tried to be a great role model to him. Isn't that what every parent strives for, to lay down good examples for their children? But I knew that my drinking was setting a terrible example. Even though I felt like a great dad in many other areas of my life, drinking alcohol totally let me down, and let him down.

I had always experienced hangovers and days when I was so sick from drinking that I just wanted to curl up into a ball and do nothing, waiting for bedtime so I could get that day over with. With an average of 27,500 days in a lifetime, what a complete waste those days were. But my health was really starting to take a downward turn. The more I drank, the worse the hangovers were getting. Sometimes, they were lasting more than a day, going into two and even three days. Even drinking to cure the hangover was not helping anymore; it was barely taking the edge off. When I woke in the morning after a big drinking session, I felt like I was dying, literally. I knew that if I kept using this drug, I'd eventually need to drink in the morning, just to get through my life.

I finally came to the conclusion that whatever it took to get over this bad habit had to be better than what I was going through each and every day. And I was right! Fortunately, my symptoms were nowhere near what I had imagined they would be like.

You Are Here

If you feel afraid of crossing your starting line on this alcohol freedom journey, spend some time thinking about where you are now. Look at how bad your hangovers have become. Be very clear with yourself that they are never going to improve. The more you drink, the worse your hangovers will become.

Think about your health, as it stands now. How much has it deteriorated over the last few years? Think about your relationships as they stand now. How have they been affected over the years? Think about as many aspects of your life as you can in this way.

Once you do that, you are in a good place to start making comparisons.

The Symptoms and Side Effects of My Drinking!

"Only two things are infinite, the universe and human stupidity, and I'm not sure about the former."
Albert Einstein

Sleeping With the Enemy

By the time I knew it was time to stop, my drinking was definitely taking the best out of me. I don't think I'd had a sound sleep in years, not since I had quit back in 2008. Most nights I would drink enough alcohol so that when my head hit the pillow I would be comatose very quickly. If I didn't drink, I'd end up tossing and turning for what seemed like hours, waiting for sleep to come.

When I went to bed drunk, my body would just shut down. It was almost like flicking a switch and all the lights going out. Of course, this was the most efficient way that my body had of dealing with the poison that I kept pouring in, night after night. The body mission was simple, knock out the idiot, only keep the essential life support ticking over, and then get to work on damage limitation.

I almost never lasted the whole night through, mostly waking up after 4-5 hours of so-called sleep. Then I would just lay there, feeling like crap. All the numbing effects of the alcohol had worn off leaving my head buzzing and my body aching and ill. In the quiet bedroom, over the soft sounds of my partner next to me, I would hear the BOOM BOOM BOOM of my heart pounding in my ears. It felt like it was going to hop out of my chest, my head banging to the same insane rhythm. My mouth parched, despite the gallons of beer I'd swigged the night before. Completely dehydrated and needing to hold onto as much liquid as possible, the diuretic effect of the alcohol would continue sending wrong signals to my kidneys ... get rid of more water. And my bladder would only be too happy to oblige.

Every organ in my body ached. Everything gets screwed up with alcohol poisoning, or the hangover, as we like to call it. The body is put under immense pressure to eliminate the poison as quickly as possible. It's called the desire to live. When we drink alcohol, we put our body systems into survival mode, it's a life or death situation every night. All the other tasks your poor body is supposed to get on with are forgotten about, or given half-assed attention at best.

Payback

Once I was awake, listening to that frightening pounding sound hammering through my body, I found it hard getting back to sleep. All the 'fun' of the instant gratification was gone. Now it was time to pay the cost.

If by chance I did get back to sleep, I'd only be delaying the inevitable sickness by a couple of hours of agitated unrest. As I said, usually all chance of sleep was gone. I usually got up so as not to wake my soundly sleeping partner, Esther. Sometimes just had to get up because I was too scared to stay laying in the dark.

I normally spent the day in a sort of twilight zone. I wouldn't, or couldn't work! Feeling sorry for myself was my default state of mind. Sorry for drinking so much. Sorry for feeling so bad. Sorry for me! I would most likely curl up on the couch, in front of the computer, or just sit on the balcony staring into space, watching the world blissfully going about its own business. It all amounted to the same thing ... doing as little as possible, achieving nothing, and letting the day slowly seep away!

At this stage, most of my hangovers were taking two or three days to clear. But the fact is, I never allowed them to completely clear up. By the time the evening came, I would be drinking again. At best, if I couldn't stomach any more booze (which was rare), I'd wait until the next day. I was on a continuous cycle of drink - drunk - detox - drink - drunk - detox - and on and on - forever spinning around and around.

The hangovers felt like I had a bad flu. Nausea, sometimes vomiting, very sweaty, headaches, pain all through my body, kidney pain, liver pain, joint pain. Brain dead! Staring into space like a zombie. Zombified! My only ambition was to get to tomorrow as fast as possible. My brain felt like it was wrapped in a heavy cold, wet towel, without any of the soft comfort.

Before and After

Now I'm in a position to make comparisons between before and after. All the symptoms and the side effects and the cravings, all the unpleasantness, all the discomfort that I went through in those first few days after I had stopped poisoning myself, were all a walk in the park compared to the symptoms, side effects, and cravings, the cruel self-inflicted punishments and pain that I had been feeling for all those years!

Of course, it took time for my body and brain to adjust. It took time for the alcohol to be completely gone from my system. However, I was feeling physically good within a couple of days. I knew that once I stopped, I'd have to go through that one last hangover, completely through it this time, no matter how long it took. As I've said, my hangovers were starting to last a few days.

I often look back to the first video I made for alcoholmastery.com, Video Journal 1*, in the first week after I quit. Looking at it now reminds me of the sorry person I used to be. It's a snapshot of what my life looks like as a drinker. A very stark warning of what's waiting for me if I ever decide to revisit my weak old self. I see a bloated and ill guy, someone that I remember very well. Most of the time I want to forget that time. But it's good to remember just who I was. The first time I replayed the video, the thing that most struck me was the sadness in my eyes.
It's a place I'm never going back to!

*http://alcoholmastery.com/welcome-to-alcohol-mastery-video-journal-1/

My Quit

"I don't seek discomfort. But, very often, you realise that what you fear is actually quite ephemeral; something's different, something's unfamiliar; therefore, it must be worse."
Michael Palin

Finding Pink Elephants

Once I had made up my mind to quit, I thought a lot about the idea of never having a drink again. Although those thoughts were intimidating, I was able to push them to the back of my mind because I was in the first flush of my determination. I was sick of drinking. I never wanted to see the stuff again. Alcohol was the cause of the mess I found myself in right now.

The thoughts I couldn't escape as easily were about what would happen to me over next few days and weeks. One part of me was elated about this new life, yet another part was terrified. I had a torrent of questions and not many answers.

How would I react? How would I relax, or stress relieve, or party, or function without the numbing effects of booze? How would others would react to me? Would they think I was an alcoholic? How would my body cope? Was my mind strong enough? Did I have the determination to see me through?

I had quit drinking for 10 months a few years before, and I didn't remember any bad symptoms or side effects back then, but now I had 5 years more drinking under my belt. What if my body was not as forgiving this time around? Would it be more painful? I used to smoke and overcoming that habit was one of the hardest things I've ever done. It had taken me so many attempts. Would it be the same with drinking?

I had no-one that I could turn to for advice. I didn't know anyone who had quit drinking for good, nobody I could talk to at any rate.

In the circumstances, I did what most people would do, I opened my web browser and started searching.

I read and re-read everything I could find. I was a passive observer on quit alcohol forums. I read articles and stories on medical websites, blogs, encyclopedias, news sites, and so on. By the time I had finished, I was more confused and overwhelmed than ever. For some people, quitting was easy - for others, it turned into a life-long battle. Alcoholism was a disease and it wasn't a disease. One website told you to seek urgent medical help, another that you could do this on your own. Nothing was clear! Everything was contradictory! I was confused and uncertain about what was going to happen and what was the best path to take. Everything I had read online, in my perception, only prepared me to expect the worst.

Thankfully, I was wrong.

Despite winding myself up for the worst possible results, the only real "symptom" I experienced was difficulty sleeping. I had a little shakiness as well, but that was because my body and brain were rattled by all the boozing. The only thing I experienced, in those first few days, was the hangover.

Finding Sleep

It did take about a month before I slept properly. I should say it took about a month to go from hardly any sleep to having a great sleep and feeling entirely rested when I woke in the morning.

The first few days were the most challenging. Reading has always been a big part of my bedtime routine. Being drunk and reading don't always go hand in hand. The first requirement of reading is to be able to see the words on the page. My normal bedtime ritual was to wait until I felt sleepy enough to go to bed, usually aided by the alcohol. Then I'd get into bed, open a book, read two or three paragraphs, and I'd be quickly away to la la land!

In those first few days, my bedtime routine was missing one essential element, the alcohol sledgehammer. I got into bed, opened my book and read… and read… and read. My eyes got heavy, I'd put down the book, ready for sleep, and as soon as I turned out the light I was wide awake again. After a couple of hours of this torment, I finally dozed off into a kind of fitful twilight zone. You couldn't really call it sleep.

Gradually, as my body got used to the idea that no more alcohol was forthcoming, falling asleep got easier and easier. It still took a few more practice runs before I could stay asleep for more than a few hours, but I got there in the end. For the first time in a very long time, I was getting a complete rest every night. Even my dreams came back. I used to have dreams when I was using alcohol, but they felt like I was viewing them with my head stuck in a fish bowl. Most of the time, I couldn't even remember what they were about. Now I was having proper vivid dreams, good dreams that I liked and wanted to remember.

When you get to this stage of normal unaided sleep, you will realize that you have not slept properly in years. Alcohol doesn't make a great sleeping aid. Although you might fall asleep quickly, the alcohol prevents you from reaching levels of sleep that are necessary for proper rest and recuperation.

The Battle for Mind

The battle of my mind took a bit longer to win. I shouldn't call it a battle because I was enjoying it. As you'll see, most of my effort would not go into wondering how I would ever survive without alcohol, it was how I could fill the vacant gaps that had suddenly opened up in my daily life. I used to drink a lot. I drank most evenings and every weekend. Now I had to fill those empty spaces without going mad!

Finding Perspective

"When you can imagine you begin to create and when you begin to create you realize that you can create a world that you prefer to live in, rather than a world that you're suffering in."
Ben Okri

You Are Here

One of the most difficult parts of this journey is making the start. How do you find the courage to cross that line? How do you minimize the fear and maximize your resolve and determination to take that first step? I believe that you achieve these things by first getting a solid grasp on *your own perspective*. You must understand where you are now and how you got here. How can you know where you are going unless you know from where you're starting?

More importantly, you need to look at both possible futures that are waiting for you. We looked at one aspect of this earlier, making comparisons between your before and after. From another perspective, what kind of future are you traveling into if you continue to drink? And, what kind of future awaits you once you stop drinking?

Visualize Your Future

A very powerful motivator is visualizing your future self. Try to imagine yourself in the shoes of the person you will become if you don't stop poisoning yourself and your life. See and feel what it's like to be the *you* of ten years into the future. Look at the people you are closest to and how they are reacting towards you. Try to look at your future self from as many different angles as you can.

- How much are you drinking?
- How often are you drinking?
- How is your family life being affected?
- What about your job or business?
- What kind of financial problems are you having?
- How do you fit in your community?
- How is your health being affected?

The Immortal Alcoholic

A couple of months before I quit, I found a website called The Immortal Alcoholic. It was one of the good things that came out of my internet searching. The blog is written by a lady who is caring for her husband, an end-stage alcoholic. In one particularly poignant post, she describes what an alcoholic death looks like. She recounts walking into her husband's room. He's lying in a bed, ill and frail, almost childlike. He can hardly speak, let alone move. In the post she recounts, "There is an odor about him that is so distasteful that it makes me back up when I get near him and couldn't approach him because of the smell."

That one sentence hit me hard. The person she was describing could be the future me! The thought of wanting to comfort someone you love, but you can't get close enough to hug them or care for them because they smell so bad. It's a scene that I'd later use to great effect in my own visualizations.

Let's get real about binge drinking or heavy drinking or alcoholism. When you are caring for someone who is suffering from Alzheimer's or Parkinson's disease, you know that they have done nothing to contribute to that condition. They are helpless in every aspect of their disease. This "disease", known as alcoholism, is completely self-inflicted. It's a condition that can be prevented. When looking at Riley, The Immortal Alcoholic himself, you know that every drink he has taken throughout his life, every selfish mouthful, has led him to this place where he is incapable of looking after himself. That dirty job is left to someone else, to his wife. I felt so sorry for her. For him, I felt only anger.

Making Me Think

Linda, the blogger behind The Immortal Alcoholic, may be waiting for the inevitable to happen with her husband. But I want her to know that she has made a big impact on me. Her story allowed me to see things from a completely different perspective. Her posts forced me to look at my alcohol use objectively, from the context of a selfish and self-indulgent waste of life. For the first time ever, I began to understand how my drinking was affecting the people that I love. I could see how my drinking was going to profoundly and negatively alter the course of their lives, as well as mine. Up until now, I had imagined that the influence my drinking had on others was fairly benign. I would make them laugh while I was drunk and acting stupid. I was that 'friendly drunk' who just talked more and acted a bit goofy.

Linda played a large part in starting to open my eyes to my inescapable downfall. If I was feeling like crap now, if my life felt wasted now, what of my future? Through these stories, I got a glimpse into the nightmare that was waiting for me if I kept pandering to my greed for instant gratification. I started to see the possible impact on the people I love, those who would have to take care of my future self. Would they even want to take care of me? Would they care enough about me, overlooking what I had done to myself, to want to burden themselves with my care? Would they have the stomach to stick around? Would I want to force that decision on them?

I'll share with you one of my most powerful visualizations, one that used to strike appalling fear into the pit of my stomach.

I imagine what it's like for my son to see me in the same situation that faced Linda as she stands over her bed ridden husband. I visualize Sean coming into my room and I am very ill. I see his face as he tries to get close to me. He wants to hug me, but at the same time he's trying to hide his disgust at how badly I smell. As I look into his eyes from my sick bed, I feel the full shame and disgust at what I have done to myself, how I have let myself descend into this pitiful existence. I think back to the way Sean used to look up at me when he was a little boy, those big blue eyes and his curly blond hair, entrusting me with everything, giving me so much unconditional love. In that child's eyes, I can do no wrong. Yet here I am, stinking up the place and killing myself slowly.

Even now, writing this, I feel a sickening jolt as that scene plays out in my mind. Use your imagination well. It is a very powerful tool.

Glimpses of Your Future

Your mind is your greatest ally. You can massively increase your chances of success by using your natural gifts for visualization to conjure up your own "what if" scenarios about your future. Try to see the inevitable consequences if you continue on this pathway of poisoning your body. At the same time, realize that it is never too late for you to change. Facing your future in this way could very well save your life. It won't cost you anything except maybe a few tears.

When you visualize this inevitable future pain and force yourself to confront the end result of your drinking, you gift yourself a very powerful and abiding motivation for change. You will find it very difficult to ignore such emotional visualizations.

As an example of using this technique, take yourself on a journey, like the one Scrooge was subjected to in the Charles Dickens novel, A *Christmas Carol*. Visualize where you've come from, who you used to be, see the person who used to smile and jump and laugh. See that person whose life didn't revolve around booze and getting drunk. Now see your present life. See yourself truly for what you are now. No bullshit! Look at how you are squandering your precious years because you want the instant indulgence of getting wasted on a drug? Finally, take yourself on that trip into your future, and see how it all ends!

These visualizations don't take long. We're talking about moments. However, these can be the most important moments you might ever spend in your life.

A Year and a Half through My Journey

"Regret is the worst human emotion. If you took another road, you might have fallen off a cliff. I'm content."
William Shatner

How Did I Get Here?

In the first few months after I had finally quit alcohol, I would often ask myself *How did I ever get into that state?*

After a year and a half, I have a much better understanding.

When we are young, we have no real concept of the dangers involved in drinking alcohol. We are taught to look left and right when we cross the road. We are taught which are the highest mountains and the longest rivers, the capital cities of our respective countries, and the greatness of the heroes and pioneers who preceded us. We are educated in history, economics, religion, philosophy, and geography. We are schooled not to take sweets from strangers, not to spit or swear, to tuck our shirts into our pants, and to have respect for our elders.

Missing Lessons

We are also drilled not to mess with drugs. We learn that drugs are dangerous, drugs are for losers, and drugs will ruin our lives!

At the same time, we teach our children that drinking alcohol is normal. Even though we have rules which govern the sale and use of alcohol before a certain age, once our kids reach that minimum age, most of the rules stop … except don't become an alcoholic.

This is not in the least bit surprising. Alcohol users are everywhere! They are the politicians who make the rules. They are the police and judges who enforce those rules. They are the businessmen who make the drinks and the doctors and nurses who treat the drunks.

And they are the professors and the teachers who educate and guide our children. It is virtually impossible to properly teach our kids on the dangers of taking this drug when so many people from all walks of life are addicted to its use.

Our Fantasy World

Our children live in a world where the Bogeyman, Santa Claus, the Tooth Fairy, and the Easter Bunny are very much real; where the alcoholic is the dirty man in the dirty coat who sleeps in on the dirty ground in a shop doorway, shooed away each morning by a disgruntled member of staff.

We live in a world where some drug dealers and drug users are evil scumbags who deserve nothing better than to be locked up, while other drug dealers and drug users (the white collar type that deal in and use alcohol) are held up as paragons of virtue and taste.

By the time our children become adults, by the time they can legally purchase alcohol, we may well have taught some important alcohol lessons. We might have told them how to be careful when drinking. We might have taught them not to drink on an empty stomach, to keep away from shots, and never, ever drink and drive. But we fail to teach the biggest alcohol lesson of all: that alcohol is a harmful drug!

It's a Drink!

We fail in this because, even though alcohol is a drug, and one of the most harmful, we don't classify it as a drug. If it's not classified as a drug, even though it has all the destructive hallmarks of a dangerous drug, how can it *be* a drug?

As a consequence, our children go through their early lives accepting alcohol as just another commodity, another drink like cola. If they get into trouble because they're drinking too much, they are given the advice to moderate, to act responsibly. This advice only adds to the normalization of alcohol use. Moderation and responsibility are not words you would ever use while advising a heroin or cocaine user. But alcohol is not perceived as a drug, like heroin or cocaine, it's perceived as a drink. What could be more normal or natural than taking a drink?

And as we've seen, when you hold your head above the parapet and say you're going to quit, that is when you are most in danger of being labeled an alcoholic, as someone who has a problem. Not before you've quit. Not during all those times when you were pouring this poison into your body. You only have a problem now that you've stopped or are trying to stop.

Trouble Just Arrived

One day you find that you have a problem with alcohol. Going by the dictates of our society, by wising up to what you're doing to yourself, you identify yourself as a possible alcoholic. You are in trouble and you don't really understand how you got there.

Each bad alcohol habit has been built up by drinking one mouthful at a time. That's how it works. You drink one mouthful after another. You have one drunken night after another. You drink one weekend after another. Soon you are drinking almost every night. Then you *are* drinking every night. Then you start to drink during the day; then earlier and earlier in the day. Finally, you just can't face life without drinking alcohol.

Telling the Truth

What would happen if everyone was told the truth about alcohol *before* they started drinking?

If you knew that you were taking a drug, would you have acted with more caution? Would the adults around you have acted with more responsibility before giving you your first drink?

If you knew alcohol was a drug, just like heroin, cocaine, angel dust, or crack, and that by taking this drug you would be a user, just like any other drug user, and that you had a chance of getting addicted to this drug, just like any other drug addict, would you have acted with more caution?

If you knew alcohol was a drug, would you still use it in front of your children?

Now you know that alcohol is a drug, at least you know what you're dealing with. Will you change your behavior?

Breaking Habits

One of the vital lessons that I've learned, since I stopped drinking alcohol, is that addiction is just another word for a bad habit. The internal processes that built my alcohol drinking habit over the years, are the same processes that I used to break the habit down once I stopped.

Breaking any habit boils down to making small and continuous adjustments in your thoughts and actions. Then you create a new set of thoughts and actions to replace the old ones. These new thoughts and actions build into a set of new habits. This process will take time. Breaking old habits and building new habits will cause discomfort, but the process is simple in that it only involves making one small adjustment after another.
Change is an inevitable part of life, it's going to happen whether you like it or not, whether you take control of those changes or not.

Instead of letting the change happen *to* you, steer your own changes in the direction that you want them to go.

The Drinking Disease

"There are two primary choices in life: to accept conditions as they exist, or accept the responsibility for changing them."
Denis Waitley

It's A Control Thing

If you perceive this habit as a disease you push the control completely out of your own hands.

If you believe you were born with alcoholism, or addiction in your genes, you are handicapping yourself from the very beginning.

How can you eliminate a gene from your body and start again? You can't! You are doomed to have this anchor around your neck for the remainder of your life.

Alternatively, what happens if you choose to see this, or any addiction, as a bad habit?

Can you see how much more powerful it is to approach any of life's challenges from the perspective that it was your thoughts and behaviors that got you into this position in the first place, and it's your thoughts and behaviors that are going to get you out of it again?

Your Ability to Respond

When you look at your alcohol drinking from this mindset, there is no blame, there is only responsibility.

Take a look at the word "responsible". It is made up from two parts, the word "response" and the suffix "-ible" or "-able". It means your ability to respond.

Where is your ability to respond to having an alcohol problem, an alcoholic addiction, or an alcohol habit if you are the victim of a disease or your genes?

If you have a disease, surely you are not in a position to respond. If alcoholism is a disease, surely it's beyond your control.

Many people go through their whole lives viewing the world from this perspective. Instead of looking for places where they can take control and actively create changes to their thinking, their behavior, or their environment, they look for the excuses, the reasons why they cannot do something, or the defects in their own ability.

They go through life with such thoughts as:

- *It's beyond my control.*
- *It's a disease and I can't help it.*
- *That's just the way things are!*
- *No matter how hard I try, I'll always fail… It's in my genes.*
- *If I say I don't drink, people will make fun of me.*
- *How comes I can't just be normal.*

Take complete control of yourself by refusing to handicap your efforts through entertaining the disease or gene perception. Take responsibility for your own actions, 100% responsibility. You are where you are because this is a habit that you and only you have created. With the right set of tools you can unmake any habit. You are in complete control and that's the best place to be!

Chapter Five - Recovery

"Tomorrow is the most important thing in life. Comes into us at midnight very clean. It's perfect when it arrives and it puts itself in our hands. It hopes we've learned something from yesterday."
John Wayne

The Recovery Process

I spoke about recovery earlier in this book. Before we delve deeper into what recovery is, here's a quick recap of what we've learned so far.

Recovery is not a place or state you are locked into after you stop drinking. It is certainly not a place you will remain for the rest of your life.

Recovery is a dynamic process of healing, much like the process you go through when you've broken a bone. It's a process with a beginning, middle, and an end. The process of healing has at its end the state of being healed.

In the next couple of sections, we'll go through the two types of recovery that are linked to quitting drinking, as I see them. First, we will look at the day-to-day cyclical recovery that every heavy drinker has to go through in order to survive. Then we'll take a look at breakout recovery, the processes your body and mind will go through once you've stopped the flow of alcohol.

Cyclical Recovery

"Do something today that your future self will thank you for!"
Unknown

Never Ending Cycle

Cyclical recovery is the process your body and mind goes through every time you take alcohol, or any other drug, into your body. As long as you're a user, your body will be stuck in this never-ending cycle of intoxication and recovery.

Think about this for a moment. Alcohol is a toxin, hence the word intoxicated. Your body deals with all toxins in the same way. There might be different degrees of alarm for different toxic substances, but the processes are essentially the same. I'm not an expert in the science of what goes on, I'm not sure there is such a thing, but I'm certainly expert in how my body felt while it was under this form of alert condition. As long as there is alcohol floating around your body, your defenses are permanently switched on.

Our culture may look upon alcohol as a way of getting drunk, having fun, or getting a buzz. Your body only sees the alcohol in one way: as a poison. Your body views alcohol as something to eliminate as quickly as possible.

As soon as alcohol enters your bloodstream, and for as long as it remains in your body, your defenses will try to limit how far the toxin can travel, reduce the overall damage caused by the toxin, and transform or eliminate the toxin from your body.

Liver Capability

The human liver can only physically handle one unit of alcohol per hour. One unit of alcohol is the size of a small glass of wine or half a pint of beer. It's not very much. In terms of alcohol found in the wild, this capacity is more than enough.

Your liver has evolved to deal efficiently with naturally occurring alcohol. Primarily, naturally occurring alcohol can be manufactured inside your body through normal digestive processes. Your liver can also deal with most alcohols naturally found in your environment, like the small amounts of alcohol we might consume in overripe fruits, and so on.

However, your liver has not evolved the ability to handle the huge doses of toxins which are found in commercially produced alcoholic drinks.

Resting Your Liver

If you're a heavy drinker, your liver never gets a real break. As soon as it gets to work dealing with the first unit, a second arrives, then a third, and so on. Your body does not have a staging or holding area where all the incoming alcohol can be stored temporarily while waiting patiently to be processed. Your mighty liver has no choice but to allow the alcohol overload to flood your network of veins and arteries, saturating your system from your feet to your brain.

If you use alcohol every day, does your liver ever get to rest? Does your liver ever get the chance to concentrate completely on the normal filtering processes that it needs to focus on, to ensure your fitness and survival?

Not really for the heavy drinker! This process of alcohol toxin elimination is constant. It becomes a never ending cycle.

Constant Damage Limitation

"Healing doesn't mean the damage never existed... it means that the damage no longer control our lives."
Unknown

When I was drinking alcohol, especially in the latter years, there was always alcohol in my body, even if I hadn't drunk it for a couple of days. My body was in what I call constant damage limitation mode. If you are a heavy drinker, your body is also going through this same constant damage limitation process all the time. While your body is tackling the alcohol, it can't make all the other repairs that need to be made. Not only are you causing direct damage to your liver and other organs through your alcohol use, there is also the indirect damage caused because the other parts of your body are not getting the necessary levels of protection and maintenance.

The cycle is always the same: Drink - Recover - Drink - Recover - Drink - Recover - Drink …

Then I Really Stopped Drinking

Once I stopped drinking for good, for the first time in a long time my body was able to move past the cyclical recovery. My breakout recovery drive kicked in and my protective systems were finally able to tackle the underlying damage that had been caused by many years of this alcoholic assault.

Think about the condition your body must be in after all these years of consistent heavy drinking. Your defense system has had to deal with the regular flood of alcohol toxins that you have thrust upon it, as well as taking care of the day to day contamination that comes from just being alive in the modern world, contamination from the air, your food, your fingers, and so on.

Then suddenly the alcohol stops. You have taken one last binge and finally you decide that enough is enough!

At Last

Of course, your body doesn't know that the toxic tap has been turned off permanently. Not in the first few days, at least. It goes through the same recovery cycle that it's gone through a thousand of time in the past. It deals with the toxins at one unit per hour as normal, breaking them down, and spitting them out. You go through the same hangover feelings that you've gone through time and again.

Only this time it's different because the flow never restarts. Your repair system can finally put all its energy into cleaning up the last dregs of alcohol. Once the final alcoholic mop-up has been completed, your body can concentrate its resources on repair and regeneration.

It won't take very long before you start to feel the difference, and this is only the beginning. The best part is you don't have to do a thing. The breakout recovery all takes place behind the scenes, while you are sorting out your head, while you are sleeping, and while you are planning for your new bright future.

Breakout Recovery

"Responsibility is the price of freedom."
Elbert Hubbard

Freedom

Once you get over the initial hangover, you're probably heading into territory you haven't been in for a long time. When I stopped drinking, I had been in that damage limitation recovery cycle for over five years. In that time, I don't think I ever went more than two or three days without my normal fix. Breaking out of that cycle felt weird but fantastic.

Contrary to what some people in quit alcohol circles will have you believe, this breakout recovery process is not an alcoholic limbo that you'll be stuck in for the rest of your life. Your recovery kicks off as soon as you stop drinking and it chugs along below the surface until you reach the state of being recovered.

Your body will finally be able function as it's supposed to function.

Recovered

As I have already said, breakout recovery is a dynamic process. Unlike cyclical recovery, breakout recovery has a beginning, a middle, and an end. You must let nature take its course. There is no magic pill that will accelerate the process. Your recovery might take a few weeks or maybe a few months. But before long, your body and mind will be once again operating at normal levels.

Instead of all the destruction you have been heaping onto your body, you now have the chance of building a better version of yourself. You will have a body and mind that can achieve the things you want to achieve in this life, not one that's being held back by drugs. Breakout recovery is a steady process that must run its course. However, you can help the process along by providing the right fuel.

Fueling Your Body's Capacity to Heal

"If we could give every individual the right amount of nourishment and exercise, not too little and not too much, we would have found the safest way to health."
Hippocrates

Fuel 1: Self-Belief

Most of the healing and rebuilding that will happen over the coming weeks and months, will happen underneath the surface of your awareness. You can help that healing and rebuilding by providing your body with the right types of fuel for the job.

I know it sounds a little corny, but the first type of self-help fuel is self-belief. You must believe that your body is capable of making these changes. After all the crap that you have put your body through in the past, you are still alive. That fact alone is a testament to your body's great inner strength. One of the biggest barriers to change is not having the belief that you can effect a change or maintain the changes once the process has begun. Your body has evolved to be strong. As you already know, your body can put up with all kinds of abuse. You need to maintain your mental strength to help your body. This brings us onto the next fuel.

Fuel 2: Nutrition

If you quit drinking and only feed yourself a diet of McDonald's hamburgers and cola, you are hindering the whole process, not helping it. "You are what you eat" may be a cliché, but it's very true. If you eat burgers and fries and cola, that's what you are going to be made of. The food that you put into your mouth ends up being the building blocks that your system will use to rebuild, to repair, to think, and to act. Do you really want to be made from burger "meat," fries, and sugar water? Is that what you deserve? It's certainly not what your body needs.

Your body needs plenty of fresh, clean water. It needs a diet that is rich in natural whole foods like fruits and vegetables, complex carbohydrates like whole grain bread, whole wheat pasta, or brown rice. Your body needs proteins that can be found in meat, vegetables, fruit, nuts, grains, or beans. If you eat meat, stick to the leaner cuts. Choose white meat over red, and avoid high cholesterol fats. You should also take a multi-vitamin supplement in the early days. Consider this an insurance, just to make sure you're really getting everything you need.

Remember: how quickly your body heals depends a lot on the fuel on which it runs. That fuel is made up of the raw ingredients you put into your body.

Fuel 3: Exercise

The third type of fuel is exercise. Exercise revs you up. If you mix exercise with the other two fuels, good thoughts and good food, you'll have more energy and improve your overall mood.

I always feel better on the days I exercise than on the days when I don't bother. Even if I feel like crap in the morning when I get out of bed, once I get into the open air and start moving, I always feel better, always! It's the same in the evening. I can have the most draining day ever, I can feel completely exhausted, but if I get out of the house and take a quick walk it makes me feel better in no time, every time. Exercise will re-energizes you. I'm not saying you have to spend an hour or two walking, that is just the routine that fits into my lifestyle. You choose the type of exercise that helps you. Choose the type of exercise that makes you feel good, that gets you moving.

Exercise will also help your body to recover. Movement helps everything work better and more efficiently. It can help your mind to remain focused and to avoid thinking about the negative aspects of quitting drinking. Oh, and don't forget your rest days. You need those as well. Don't try to overdo things. Your rest day should still have a little exercise, maybe a stroll instead of a vigorous walk, a dance instead of a run.

The Vigorous Cycle

These three elements - self-belief, nutrition, and exercise - are a complete formula for helping your body to repair, rejuvenate, and ultimately maintain a healthy balance throughout your life. Each part of this formula adds fuel to a simple vigorous cycle. By nurturing your self-belief, eating well, and getting your butt up and moving, you are helping to accelerate your recovery.

In the long term, this simple vigorous cycle formula will help you to achieve a much more fulfilled life. Your thoughts will be much more positive because your mind is being fueled by eating the proper food and getting healthy doses of oxygen from your workouts. You will make better choices about food and exercise because your thinking is now much clearer. And you will have the energy and stamina to maintain your workouts because you are strengthening your thought patterns and eating the right types of food. Each part of the cycle helps the next.

The Body in Balance

"Man maintains his balance, poise, and sense of security only as he is moving forward."
Maxwell Maltz

How Long Does Recovery Take?

One of the most frequent questions I get asked on the website is *How long will my recovery take?* There is no real answer to this. You breakout recovery will take as long as it takes. It depends on so many different factors, including how much time and effort you are willing to put into your vigorous cycle fueling.

Your body loves balance. It wants nothing more than to run at its fittest levels. Some days you will feel great, other days you won't feel so hot; but, in general, there is a set-point around which your body thrives. This process is called homeostasis. Even when you're fully dependent on drugs, your system will still try to find a balance.

Once you have quit drinking, it's almost inevitable that the processes of recovery will cause some discomfort. This physical discomfort is individual to you and no two people will go through the same experiences, so I can't tell you how you are going to feel. One thing is for sure, all your feelings of discomfort will pass. I'll talk a bit more about how you can handle this discomfort later.

Balance Restoration

Your system wants to restore the balance as soon as possible. We humans are wired for a time and place that has long disappeared. Our primal instincts and abilities have been honed over millions of years to protect ourselves and our families against the fangs and claws of large predators.

You can't run or protect yourself from the fangs and claws of a sabre-toothed tiger if your basic balances are out of whack. Even though we no longer have anything to fear from large predators, our systems are still geared to operate under those primitive conditions and with those threats being imminent. From a pure survival point of view, your body needs to restore healthy and balanced levels as soon as possible.

My Own Worst Enemy No More

Before I quit, my body felt like it was permanently exhausted. I was in pain, I was overweight, and I felt chronically ill. After I stopped drinking, it took a while before things got back into balance again. My liver pains were one of the first things to disappear. Obviously there were no more hangovers, which was very welcome.

I definitely helped the process along because no matter what happened I wasn't going to drink again, ever! I was determined to get alcohol out of my life permanently, to rebuild my life into something about which I could be proud, and above all to be the best role model I could be for my son. I changed my diet to include a lot more whole foods and eliminated a lot of the junk. I have had slip-ups on the way, but that's part of the journey. It is not in making mistakes that your journey is defined, but in how you deal with those mistakes. Mistakes are inevitable. Accept them, learn from them, and move on.

The main thing for me has always been to stop being my own worst enemy. I understand now that if I want to lead a happy, healthy, and self-fulfilled life, I have to pay the price up front, not somewhere down the line.

Your Body Immigration Officers

"Garbage in garbage out"
George Fuechsel

You Are What You Eat!

Here's one of the best explanations of the maxim *"you are what you eat"* that I have ever come across. This is from a video on Youtube by an Indian spiritual teacher called Sri Swami Satchidananda. You can watch the video here*.

He talks about the three monkeys: see no evil, hear no evil, and speak no evil. If we think about our bodies as a country, he says, our senses can be thought of as our internal immigration officers.

These immigration officers are waiting to check everything that comes into your country.

Your eyes are your first immigration officer. When you want to take a drink of water, your eyes will look over the water and say, *Yeah, it looks clear. It doesn't look like there's any dirt in it, that's okay to drink.*

Then the water is passed to the next immigration officer, your nose, which is conveniently placed just over your mouth and under your eyes. Anything that wants to go into your mouth must first pass under the scrutiny of this tough inspector. You pass the glass of water under your nose and you smell it; this immigration officer says, *yes, it smells good, it doesn't smell bad, so all is good.* It passes the second test.

The mouth is the third immigration officer. You sip the water and roll it around inside your mouth, having a good taste. This immigration officer says, *the water tastes good, it tastes like water should taste.* It passes the test and you can swallow it.

Once it passes the taste test, it flows down your throat where it meets the ultimate immigration officer, your stomach.

Satchidananda talks about how we try to fool our senses into accepting things what shouldn't be put into our bodies. We add colorings to fool the eyes. We add flavorings to fool the nose and the mouth. But the ultimate immigration officer, your stomach, is not fooled by any of these things. It says, *there is something not right about this water, get out!* Out comes the offending water the same way it came in.

Your First Alcoholic Drink

Let's examine alcohol from this perspective. When you first drink alcohol, you won't start with strong liquors or drinks that demand an acquired taste. You'll go for fruit-based drinks or you'll add something sugary or fruity to the alcohol before you try drinking it. By doing this, your eyes are fooled into thinking that you are drinking something delicious because it looks familiar. Your nose and mouth are fooled because it smells and tastes like something familiar.

You swallow and it lands in the domain of the ultimate immigration officer. But you cannot fool the stomach. Your stomach knows there is something very wrong with what you have just swallowed and the alcohol gets thrown right back out again.

If you think back to when you started drinking, how much of a conscious effort did it take for you to get through that first drink? Did you just take a sip or drink a full measure? How many times did you feel like vomiting in those early drinking years? How many times did you vomit? Do you remember the spinning sensation when you were drunk, like the whole world was whirling around like a crazed dervish?

The same advice has been passed down through hundreds of generations. We all understand it. You don't need a complicated celebrity diet to lose weight, you just need to eat less and exercise more. You don't need anyone to tell us how to stop drinking, you just stop doing it!

*https://www.youtube.com/watch?v=3MkwGTX0F_A

The Psychological Aspects of Quitting Drinking

"The law of harvest is to reap more than you sow. Sow an act, and you reap a habit. Sow a habit and you reap a character. Sow a character and you reap a destiny."
James Allen

Dealing with The Mind

As we've seen, the body is pretty much going to take care of the physical recovery after you have stopped the alcohol input. We have also seen that you can accelerate the recovery process by feeding yourself the right types of fuel for the job. Everything else comes down to dealing with what's going on upstairs, in your head.

At the end of the day, alcohol is a just a means to an end. It's a tool to get you to your chosen end result. And, given the right circumstances, you can replace alcohol with any other addiction.

Many people use TV as a coping strategy. They worked up about the fictional problems that faces cheap soap opera characters rather than deal with their own problems. Other people disappear from reality for a while by jumping into the world of video gaming. Many addicts amass great collections of guitars, cars, or tin cans. While others are dragged into the seedy world of internet pornography. Some people use food to feel good about themselves, gorging themselves until they can't eat another bite. For others, the addiction is chasing money, seeing how many zeroes can be added to the bottom of their bank statement.

While none of these addictions might cause the physical harm that alcohol or other drugs can inflict, they are right up there when it comes to the psychological damage that can result.

Practice Makes Perfect

To become dependent on anything takes a lot of time and practice, it doesn't just happen overnight. If you practice something enough times, it will become a habit. In certain circumstances that habit will form into an uncontrolled addiction. This is how our brains work. Forming habits is how we get things done.

Imagine for a moment a life where your mind couldn't construct any habits. Think about if you had to wake up every morning and relearn how to tie your shoe laces, or brush your teeth, or make the tea. Each of these tasks is a very simple form of habit, a learned sequence of thoughts and actions that you've performed over and over, so much so that you can do them without even thinking.

The trick to building any habit is repetition. You repeat the same process time after time after time, until it becomes automatic. This is also the trick to undoing a habit, repeating something else instead of what you want to replace.

Modeling Habits

Let's go back to the example of tying your shoelaces.

When you first attempted to tie your shoelaces, you didn't have a clue how to do it. You didn't know if the laces were arranged in your shoes correctly, you didn't know which part of the lace was supposed to go where, or the first thing about tying a proper knot.

You probably learned to tie your laces for the first time by modeling someone else, maybe your father or your older brother. They may have knelt next to you while you watched them go through the process in super slow motion, talking you through each movement they made. Maybe they taught you a little rhyme to help you to remember and practice the process.

After you had practiced going through the process a couple of times, with the help of your *"rabbit in the hole"* rhyme, you could probably fumble your way through a complete performance without any help. You still had to run each step through your mind before you could transfer the action to your fingers, but you had learned the basic technique.

Now that you have tied your shoelaces so many times that you can do it blindfolded, you don't have to think about it anymore.

A Life Full of Habits

If we didn't have this ability to habitualize such simple processes, we could never learn anything beyond the most rudimentary tasks. We wouldn't need to learn how to tie our shoe laces because there would be no such thing as shoes. If we couldn't habitualize our lives we'd still be stuck in the trees, or more likely the primordial sludge.

Everything we do is habitualized to one degree or another. Habits are the mental programming that allow us to cross the road safely, to read, to write, to speak, to play football, to dance a waltz, or any of the other million aspects of our lives that we so take for granted. Problems occur because our minds don't choose the things to habitualize based on what is good or bad, what is moral or immoral, or by what is logical or illogical.

Click Whirr - Repetition and Automaticity

How does your mind know when it's time for the habit formation cycle to begin? The basic initiator and building block of any habit is repetition. Once you repeat an action more than a few times, you establish its importance in your mind. The action might be tying your shoelaces, looking left and right before you cross the road, or becoming addicted to a drug. The action itself doesn't matter. The only thing that matters is you repeating the action. If you don't like something, you don't repeat it. It is as simple as that. The more you repeat the same pattern, the more importance you're giving it. The higher the importance, the more building blocks are used to reinforce that habit. The foundation thus becomes stronger which makes it easier and easier for you to repeat the task over and over again.

Eventually you get to the stage where you can repeat the action without conscious thought. The behavior has become sub-conscious and habitual. When you brush your teeth in the morning, are you thinking about it? This is known as automaticity. Instead of having to think about doing something, you just do it. It becomes like a program running in the background. Something will happen to *trigger* the event and, with a click and a whirr, the program automatically runs through its command cycle.

One of the secrets for fighting bad habits, and creating new good habits, is in breaking down and derailing the triggers that kick everything off.

Sensual Selves

We interact with the outside world through our senses. Information comes in through these senses, is organized and interpreted in the brain, experienced through our emotions, compared with what we've experienced before, and either acted upon or ignored.

If all you are doing is sitting in a chair, staring into space and not really thinking about much, there is still a constant inflow of information entering your mind through your senses. The majority of this activity is perceived below the surface, so you're not consciously aware of it. But just because it's not hitting your conscious mind doesn't mean it's not being assimilated into your thoughts. Your subconscious registers almost everything to one degree or another.

Mind Filters

There are many theories about the way incoming information is processed. One theory suggests that there are a series of filters which are set up between the electrical impulses arriving into your brain from the outside world and your conscious awareness. The most important information will skip through all the filters, reaching your conscious mind in a fraction of a second. Most of the information won't even get past the first filter. This is good. Most of this discarded data is just irrelevant background nonsense, the noises and the smells and images that you don't need to process. This data is acknowledged only enough so it can be ignored.

Just like habits, these filters are an essential part of who you are. If there were no such filters, everything that came in through your senses would go straight into your conscious mind. The sheer volume of information, instantly pouring into your brain, would make it impossible for you to make sense of anything. Your mind would shut down like an overloaded electrical circuit. You would end up in a padded cell.

Imagine walking down a busy main street and being consciously aware of everything. You are conscious of every person who is walking by you, every shout, every car horn, every movement, every smell, nothing is left out! What do you think that would do to your mind?

In reality, when you are in such a crowded and busy environment, your mind will register everything that's going on. But you will only be aware of a very small fraction, say 00.001%. Your awareness will always be confined to the things that are likely to directly impact you. For instance, you will notice the people who you might bump into as you make your way along the sidewalk. You will also notice any sudden or unusual sounds – like a car horn right beside you or someone shouting your name.

Awareness and perception are fascinating and very complex subjects and could fill up many volumes on their own. Suffice to say that these internal filters are absolutely essential. They make it possible for you to live and thrive in this world.

Bar Smells

Once your habits are well established, many of the moment by moment details that comprise the habit lie between these filters and won't reach your awareness.

Let's look at an example, walking into your favorite bar. Think about everything that you experience from the time you walk into the bar until the time you leave. The sound of the door creaking as it opens, the conversation of the other customers, the smell of booze and crisps and people. Think about the familiar faces of the bar staff and the other regulars. Think about the familiar greetings as you walk towards your usual spot at the bar or your preferred table. The sounds of glasses clinking, beer taps pouring, cash registers opening and closing, the background music, the sports on the TV, and so on.

Each of these individual events generally happens in the background. You don't notice any of them; they're filtered before they get to your conscious mind. When something out of the ordinary happens, you suddenly become aware of the background. You hear a glass break, someone lets out a whoop because their team has scored a goal in the match playing on the TV, the first sip of your pint tastes sour or the liquid feels too warm, or you see a cockroach scurrying across the floor.

Reminders of the Familiar

All these ordinary background events are also associations or triggers for your alcohol drinking. The pop of a cork, the crack as the seal is broken on a new bottle of spirits, or the glugging as the liquid is poured into a glass. When you go to a bar once you've stopped drinking, particularly a familiar bar, you are no longer taking part in the main action, the alcohol consumption. All your alcohol triggers will still firing off, but they are not leading to the expected conclusion, to your expected reward, feeling the effects of the alcohol in your body. Now, you cannot help but take in everything that's happening on the periphery. Everything that used to be in the background now acts as a sharp reminder of the thing that you're missing … the alcohol.

Each learned association is woven into the familiar patterns that make up your drinking environment. That drinking environment is wherever you have been used to drinking alcohol in the past. It could be your favorite bar or your favorite armchair at home. Each pattern adds a layer of complexity to your overall drinking habit. Your habits end up being the sum of all these patterns, and like most things in life, the sum often exceeds the individual parts.

Overcoming the habit means breaking these triggers.

Breaking Triggers

One method of breaking a trigger is to change the trigger meaning. You can alter the perceptions, the thoughts, and the emotions that are attached to the triggers. When I used to drink, I always associated finishing work with having a cool pint of beer. In my mind, I associated being thirsty with drinking beer. I broke this trigger by drinking water as soon as I finished work, or as soon as I was thirsty. By never allowing myself to get too thirsty, it didn't take very long to break the association between finishing work and beer drinking. I also had the bonus that my thirst was better satisfied by the water than it ever was by drinking the beer.

A second way of breaking your triggers is to manipulate your environment. For instance, you can prevent a lot of triggers from firing off in your home by getting rid of your drinking alcohol reminders. Take all the booze out of the liquor cabinet and throw it away. Get rid of the glasses, the corkscrews, the beer mats, and so on.

A third method of breaking your alcohol triggers is to change your environment. You can stop the pub triggers by not going to the pub.

You can stop other people from triggering your old habit by avoiding other drinkers for a while. And you can drive home by a different route, one that doesn't pass the liquor store/off-license or your favorite bar.

Default Behaviors

By the time we get to adulthood, most of our fundamental defaults are already in place. For many of us, it's not a question of are we going to drink, only when we are going to drink. Most of us don't question the normalcy of drinking alcohol. We don't question the intelligence of putting this poison into our bodies indefinitely. We don't view alcohol as a drug or as a poison. All that conditioning has been established a long time before we could legally buy our own booze.

Is this the fault of our parents? Yes and no! Yes, because it is the responsibility of our parents to show us the way. They're our first teachers. It's their job to give us the right tools to face the world.

My son drinks and that is partly my fault. I hate to admit that. I want to think of myself as being the model parent. How can I be a model parent when, through my own actions, I have encouraged drug use in my child? Our children learn mostly by example. Tell a child not to drink and maybe he won't. If he sees most of the grown-ups using alcohol, he'll just assume that drinking alcohol is the normal thing to do. When he is an adult, the programming will likely kick in and he will become a drinker.

In our parent's defense, they were taught the same things by their parents. Our grandparents led by example just the same as our parents did. The same as I did!

Most of our western cultures are alcoholic. It's easy to be an alcohol user if you live in an alcoholic culture. If the drug of choice was heroin, and that's not such a big leap as you might imagine, the majority of us may well be heroin users as well. If that were the case, would we also be pretending that heroin wasn't a drug?

One of the reasons people have problems quitting drinking alcohol is because they are looking in the wrong place for the culprit. They are looking at the alcohol, when the real culprit is in their own thinking and perceptions. Alcohol is only the means to an end. Once you begin to look at it from that angle, you will realize that the solution is entirely under your control. Ultimately you are responsible for making the adjustments that will bring about your change.

Changing Automaticity!

"For imagination sets the goal picture which our automatic mechanism works on. We act, or fail to act, not because of will, as is so commonly believed, but because of imagination."
Maxwell Maltz

Cutting Your Hand Off for a Smoke

A friend of mine once described to me how quitting smoking was like having his right hand chopped off. After he'd lost his familiar crutch, he felt as if he had to relearn everything.

Smoking took up a large part of his life. The first thing he did when he woke up in the morning was smoke a cigarette. It was also the last thing he did before he got back into bed at night. He smoked before and after a meal, when he was on the phone, or while he drove his car. He couldn't do without a cigarette when he was taking his lunch break, having a pint after work, or at any other time when he had a spare five minutes and wasn't restricted by the *anti-smoking police*. He smoked when he was happy, sad, or indifferent. He smoked as a distraction or to overcome his boredom. When he drank alcohol, of course he smoked twice as many cigarettes.

If you have ever had a smoking habit, you'll understand a lot of this. I can relate to it all. It took me over 100 attempts to finally quit smoking.

Relearning is Easy with a Gun to Your Head

Imagine if you had a freak accident and your dominant hand was chopped off. Everything that you take for granted in your day-to-day life suddenly becomes a struggle. Tying your shoelaces, writing, eating, cooking, catching, throwing, and playing are some of the things you will need to relearn, not to mention clapping.

We all perform our routine actions for the most part without the need to think about them. But we weren't born with these skills. Each of these rudimentary skills were gradually learned and absorbed during our childhood. The next time you get the opportunity, take a look at how a new-born baby acts. They don't even realize that those little things floating backwards and forwards in front of their faces are hands, let alone *their* hands. First they learn that those little pink things belong to them, then that they are controllable. Slowly, over many months, the baby will learn how to control them.

This point was illustrated for me a few years ago by a friend who was born without any hands. He was a victim of thalidomide. Thalidomide was a drug that had been sold in West Germany in 1957 to reduce morning sickness in pregnant mothers. Thousands of children were born with malformed limbs, a condition known as phocomelia; 60% of these children died. My buddy was one of the survivors.

One day I told him that I had great respect for him because of what he had achieved, despite his disability. He laughed. In his broad German accent he said, "What fucking choice did I have!"

This was just the way he was born. He didn't miss his hands because he never had any to start with. Each incremental skill he has learned, from the time he was born, was gained by using the tools that were at his disposal. Instead of a hand and forearm, he has a single finger just below each elbow. His biggest disability was not in his 'missing' hands, it was living in a world designed for hands. Yet this "disability" has never prevented him from doing anything. Once he has set his mind to doing something, he will always find a way of getting it done. If something doesn't work for him, he will rethink, adjust, and adapt to the situation. Quite often, this means spending some time thinking about how he can have something modified to fit him. For instance, his car is an automatic with a few minor adaptations to the steering wheel and the gear shift, making them reachable for his arms. He earns his living by playing on a modified trumpet. He earned his skippers license by adapting himself. He worked hard to get his divers license, again by self-belief and adaptation. So far, he has achieved more things in his life than most people will ever achieve, disability be damned!

Think → Adapt

His attitude is remarkable. Most people could benefit from his example. Just because something seems impossible on the surface doesn't mean it is not possible. The answers to most of life's problems can be found with a little thinking and adaptation. Most people want the world to adapt to them instead of them adapting to the world. Tough, because the world adapts to no one!

What has all this got to do with changing your drinking habit? If you lose your hands or you are quitting drinking, exactly the same systems are in play. Whether you change through your own decisions or because you have no choice in the matter, you will use the exact same tools for adjusting your life to the new set of situations.

The automaticity of any habit can be undone through your natural ability to think about change, to picture what life will be like when you change, and then to adapt and make those changes happen. Awareness of the need to change is the first step. Breaking your habit automaticity is simply about thinking and adjusting. Following that, it's about thinking and readjusting some more. The process continues, you rinse and repeat the same steps over and over until in time you replace one automatic behavior with another.

You first have to go through your changes mentally before you can do them physically. You need to think about each step in your mind before you can put it into practice.

Moving Homes

"Repetition of the same thought or physical action develops into a habit which, repeated frequently enough, becomes an automatic reflex."
Norman Vincent Peale

Smooth Sailing

Moving house is an example of the effect of automaticity that most of us have experienced at one time or other in our lives.

For instance, imagine that you are about to move house. Over the time you have lived in your present home, you have developed many routine habits in your day-to-day life. You throw your legs out of the same side of the bed each morning. You reach down and put on your slippers or your socks in the same manner, right foot then left. Then you stand up and turn to the bedroom door, which is on your right. You reach for the door handle on the left side of the door, twist the handle down, and pull the door towards you. You walk out of the bedroom, turn to the left and into your bathroom. Once in the bathroom you take a pee. The loo is on your left as you go through the bathroom door. Once you finish with that, you turn around to the washbasin behind you, which is under the mirror. As you wash your hands, you take a quick glance in the mirror, examining the reflection staring back at you, focusing on a new pimple or a long nose hair. Your toothbrush is on the shelf above the sink. You take it down and squeeze a dollop of toothpaste onto its wet bristles. As you brush your teeth, you daydream about the day ahead. You might finish up in the bathroom by washing the sleep out of your eyes and combing your hair. You leave the bathroom and make your way down the dimly lit hallway and into the kitchen, where you switch on the kettle or coffee maker, turn on the radio, and gradually come to life.

You perform this routine, along with many others, every morning before leaving for work. You go through the same things time after time and day after day. Each of these routines becomes a mini-habit.

You don't need to think about any of it, at least not consciously. You will only become conscious of an action if something out of the ordinary happens: you pee on the floor or spill coffee all over yourself. Otherwise, you could almost perform these actions in your sleep.

Where's My Bloody Coffee????

A big change is about to happen in your life, you are moving home.

Moving home is one of the most stressful times in any person's life. One of the reasons for this stress is because many of your automatic routines are non-transferable. You can't bring them with you to your new home. You'll have to relearn many things.

Let's look at your first morning in your new home. You wake up for the first time in your new bedroom. Perhaps your first thought is. *Where the hell am I?*

The first thing your sleepy head notices is that the bed is facing the wrong way. You haven't unpacked your slippers yet so they are not waiting for you as you swing your feet out onto the floor. You stand up, bursting for the morning wee, but before you move you have to first get your bearings. The door is in a completely different part of the room, so you need to think about which way you are going to move. Through the dim morning light, you spot the door and walk towards it. You automatically reach for the handle where it has always been, on the left side of the door, but your hand flaps uselessly about against the empty wood. You realize with mild annoyance that the handle is on the other side. Your bathroom is in the wrong place, as are your toilet and wash basin. Now you have to think about everything, every step of the way. Where's your toothbrush? Where's your comb? There's no towel! You'll be alright once you've had your first cup of steaming hot coffee. But where the bloody hell is the kitchen?

Of course, this feeling of confusion doesn't last long. You will soon get used to the new layout. The unfamiliar quickly becomes the familiar.

Life's New Formation

This is a very similar process to the one you will go through when you quit drinking. Many areas of your new life are going to be unfamiliar. This unfamiliarity is responsible for much of the discomfort that you will feel. Once you stop drinking, your old automatic drinking behavior is no longer being satisfied. You will feel at a loss about what to do. Quitting alcohol leaves many holes in your life that used to be filled by the drinking. Don't worry! You are designed for life-long adaptation. Just as you will quickly adapt to the layout of your new home, you will quickly adapt to the layout of your new alcohol-free life. The unfamiliar and the uncomfortable will shortly become the familiar and the comfortable. In a no time at all, you will find yourself adjusted and changed!

Chapter 6 - Mindsets

"That's been one of my mantras - focus and simplicity. Simple can be harder than complex: You have to work hard to get your thinking clean to make it simple. But it's worth it in the end because once you get there, you can move mountains."
Steve Jobs

What is a Mindset?

A mindset is an attitude or mentality that you use to deal with every aspect of your life. Each mindset is a single or set of assumptions, a frame of mind, or a belief that you have developed through your experience and learning.

One simple example is the mindset of glass half empty thinking or the glass half full thinking. The glass half empty mindset leans towards pessimistic thoughts. A glass half full mindset, on the other hands, leans more towards positive thoughts.

Fixed Vs Growth Mindsets

In her book, Mindset: The New Psychology of Success, Carol S. Dweck talks about two types of overall mindset, the fixed mindset and the growth mindset. The fixed mindset is based around the fundamental belief that you cannot change what you are born with. People with this mentality believe that they are born with a fixed quota of intelligence, talent, and so on. They further believe there is nothing they can ever do to change this fixed quota.

People with the growth mindset, on the other hand, believe that they are merely born with a starter pack of intelligence and talent. What they then do with these starter-attributes is up to them. People who have this growth mindset believe that they can cultivate their own successes, their own personalities, and their own lives.

The growth mindset is all about believing that the control buttons which can alter your life are in your hands. Over the next couple of sections, we'll take a look at some of the change mindsets that you can cultivate which will help you stop drinking for good.

Changing How You React to "Discomforts," i.e. Symptoms/Cravings/Side-Effects

"If you look for truth, you may find comfort in the end; if you look for comfort you will not get either comfort or truth only soft soap and wishful thinking to begin, and in the end, despair."
C. S. Lewis

Discomfort Mindset

Nobody likes being uncomfortable. It's not a pleasant feeling. The problem with this is that comfort can often be the enemy of change.

Our first mindset is that quitting drinking alcohol is going to cause you a little discomfort. But that's it! For most people, there's nothing heavy or life threatening about feeling uncomfortable in this way. The major battle you will have to fight is in your mind. To win this battle, you need to consistently focus your mind on thinking the right thoughts. You can overcome any discomfort with little or no fuss if you concentrate your focus on how great your life is going to be once you stop poisoning yourself with alcohol. Discard all your unnecessary thoughts about bad symptoms, bad side effects, or bad cravings. These types of negative thoughts will keep you firmly locked in the 'alcoholic' frame of mind.

If you are worried about any aspect of your health, or how quitting alcohol is going to affect your health, go to your doctor and listen to what she has to tell you. Before you quit, your aim should be to remain calm and to think logical thoughts about your new journey. Understand that although it is not going to be easy, for all the reasons we've already gone through, but each step is going to be simple.

I have already written much about the risks, so I'm not going to go into that again here. There are many people who will try to discourage you from even stepping across the starting line by telling you that nobody should attempt to quit alcohol on their own.

Don't listen to them. There are millions of people who successfully have quit alcohol - on their own. As I have already said, if in doubt visit your doctor. If they say you need medical help, fair enough. For the majority of people, this will not be needed.

The Discomfort Will Pass

The second mindset is that you will only feel the discomfort in the short term, it will pass. Accept that you're going to feel uncomfortable for a while. Then you can just ride out that discomfort. For most of us, we started drinking a long time ago. That makes it difficult to remember back to a time when we didn't drink. We have no reference point about how we should or shouldn't feel with no alcohol in our body anymore. Our lives have become deeply connected with alcohol and each of these connections can trigger the *alcohol itch*. This is merely a part of the alcohol habit. Over a short period of time, these triggers will lose their influence or the connections will become linked to something else. What you need to keep in mind is that if you don't feed the triggers, they will quickly lose their potency.

Once you get past your first month alcohol-free, you will have a better understanding about what life without alcohol feels like and what to expect in the future. Alcohol will be out of your system, your life will settle into new routines and new habits, and your sleep patterns should have stabilized. Your thoughts about alcohol will still make an appearance, but those they will occur further and further apart. Week by week and month by month you will get used to being without alcohol. Your mind is being thoroughly reprogrammed. You are building a new database of feelings, memories, thoughts, and actions associated with your new comfortable way of living.

You Hold the Discomfort Controls

The third mindset is that the level of discomfort you feel is very much within your personal control. If you dwell on how uncomfortable or how unfortunate you are, if you tell yourself that you can't stand it, or you can't do it anymore, or you that don't want to feel like this, you are being your own worst enemy.

Instead, you can choose to focus your thoughts on how these discomforting feelings are only temporary. Concentrate your thoughts on the fact that these feelings are going to decrease before eventually fading away altogether. Concentrate and focus on how good your life is now that you are free from this insane drug.

Every minute that passes signifies the evolving steps you are taking towards the person you want to be and further away from your old alcohol influenced life. Each feeling of discomfort that you accept and control adds to your stockpile of strength and fortitude.

Here's a great tip for altering how you are thinking. Get up and move. Go for a walk. Do anything that takes your mind off the negative thoughts. This works for any negativity, not just for your negative thoughts about alcohol.

When I was in those first few weeks of my journey and I found myself thinking negatively about what I was doing, I would get myself up and take a walk up and down the stairs of the apartment complex where I live. We live on the fourth floor, that's four flights or about 200 steps from bottom to top. I would climb up and down each one of those steps until I wasn't thinking about negativity anymore. I found it extremely difficult to do both things at once, being miserable about not drinking anymore and being miserable about having to walk up and down these damned steps. If you are going to feel miserable anyway, you might as well be the boss of that misery. Never let yourself wallow in self-pity. Take yourself by the scruff of the neck and force yourself to be miserable about doing something energetic. You will find, however, that this type of exercise releases some wonderful happy and natural hormones in your body.

Comparing Your Discomfort

The fourth mindset is that the amount of discomfort you will go through after you've quit is very little in comparison to what you are going through right now and nothing in comparison to the misery you are inevitably going to face if you don't change from your destructive path. Why are you quitting? You are not doing it for nothing! I quit because of the terrible pain I felt at being a bad influence on my son and the suffering of getting up every morning to a horrible hangover.

Also, think about the pain that is waiting for you if you don't stop using this drug. How will that pain compare to the discomfort you are feeling right now? Never forget that right now is the only time you get to do anything. If you are going to avoid quitting right now, when are you actually going to quit? You will eventually have to face the discomfort, one way or another. You can't do it in the future or the past. Choose to do it now! Pluck up the courage and put up with the discomfort now!

Start your discomfort comparison by thinking about the discomfort you are feeling every day because of your drinking, the mental and the physical pain. Add to that the misery and suffering that you will go through in the future if you don't stop. Now ask yourself can you afford not to quit right now? Can you afford to waste this opportunity?

Remember, the discomfort of quitting will pass with time, but the pain and suffering that you are already experiencing from using alcohol will only become worse. You are standing at a crossroads in your life. Your choice involves some pain, either way. You have to suck it up and take a few weeks of gradually decreasing discomfort before moving onwards and upwards into your new life. Or you can turn a blind eye toward your future and continue to take the destructive path of gratifying yourself in the moment. As always, the choice is yours!

The bottom line is you need to get comfortable feeling some discomfort for a while - but it is very much worth it! So do it!

Habit Memories

"A whole stack of memories never equal one little hope."
Charles M. Schulz

What is a Habit Memory?

A habit memory is a part of your old habit that has momentarily popped back into your awareness.

Although these habit memories can happen at any time, they are usually triggered by something that has just happened in your environment. They are set off by the habitual associations that you previously linked with alcohol. As I said earlier, if you've been drinking for any number of years, you'll have a lot of these triggers.

Day to Day Triggers

Many of your day to day triggers will be broken down very quickly once you've quit. The first triggers to go are those that have been consistently linked with the day-to-day parts of your life. These routine triggers include finishing work and having a beer, having a drink with a meal or while you are watching TV, or having a few drinks over the weekend while you are out with your friends.

Once you quit drinking, your day-to-day life will still happen as normal. You'll go to work in the morning and come home in the evening. You're still going to eat, watch TV, and socialize. When you constantly repeat these normal activities, day after day, the associations that these events used to have with alcohol will weaken and eventually fail because they are no longer being reinforced.

Uncommon Ambush Triggers

Habit memories, on the other hand, come from ambush triggers. These are the triggers that are associated with events in your life that don't happen every day. These are the once-a-year events like Christmas, Easter, or your birthday. Or they are the triggers that happen infrequently like office parties, weddings, christenings, funerals, and so on.

Because these events only happen occasionally, they won't have gone through the consistent repetition that you used to deal with your routine triggers, so they might not have weakened enough to break. This is not a problem; the opposite can be said about these occasional triggers. When these alcohol triggers were being constructed, they didn't have the same reinforcement as your routine triggers, so they won't be as strong in the first place.

The concern with these habit memories is they can take you by surprise. The triggers that spark off your drinking thoughts on these occasions are the ones that are unique to a particular and irregular event. Toasts at the wedding are one instance. The Christmas holiday season is another. It might be just a combination of triggers that haven't occurred at the same time since you quit. Let me give you an example.

Two Plus Two Makes Five

About ten months after I had quit alcohol, I got a phone call from a good friend who is still living in Ireland. It wasn't an unusual call, I haven't seen him since I came to Spain, but I've spoken to him several times over the phone.

It's always really great to catch up on what's going on back home. We tell each other stories about work, talk about the new Arsenal signings or how well the team is doing in the league. It's also a chance for me to catch up on what different people are doing and so on.

During this one particular call, I asked him what he was up to. He said, *"I'm in Paddy Quinn's,"* which one of our old haunts, and *"I'm on my way to the Diamond in a minute"* - which was another one of our regular spots. In that moment, it felt like no time had gone by since I'd left Ireland. I felt like I was just two miles up the road instead of two thousand miles away in a different country. I could taste the beer, smell the bar, see everything that was going on, and everyone who was in the bar. I almost said, *"I'll meet you in a while!"*

The whole conversation had evoked a vivid habit memory. The conversation involved a series of simple words that would have immediately triggered my drinking in the past. Liam would call on the phone, I'd ask him where he was, he'd tell me which bar he was in, and I'd say - *"I'll be down in a while."*

What I felt, after that phone call, was a very strong feeling of urgency and angst that lasted for a couple of minutes. I didn't know what the hell was going on at first and it took me a while to understand what had just happened. Each of the elements of the conversation was of no consequence on its own. But when all these elements were tied together the way they were, they made for a very strong alcohol triggering force. I have had these habit memories since that phone call, but at least I know what they are, and I can brush them off very easily.

Habit memories are a little overwhelming if you don't understand what's happening. It doesn't mean you're an alcoholic and it doesn't mean that you are still thinking about drinking. It's just a mind trick. But it's good to be aware that this type of thought can sneak up on you.

Benefits of Quitting

"Failure is simply the opportunity to begin again, this time more intelligently."
Henry Ford

Hitting the Restart Button

What are the real benefits of quitting drinking for you? The real value, apart from getting rid of the toxins from your body, is that you have an open road ahead of you and so many alternative directions to choose from. This is a golden opportunity for you to re-think where you want your life to go.

In a way, making such a radical change in your life means that you get the opportunity of hitting a personal restart button. You get the chance to take a long hard look at your life from close-up. This is not an opportunity that everyone gets. Think about it. If you're on automatic pilot throughout your life, it can take something pretty heavy to break the spell and force you to re-evaluate how your life is going.

New Territories

Most drinkers will go through their entire lives believing that their alcohol use is as "normal" as drinking a cup of coffee in the morning. How many people will ever view alcohol as an impediment?

You are entering new territory where you will learn how your alcohol habit works. As a bi-product of this very intimate education, you will also learn how all your habits work. As I said earlier, the principles are the same regardless of the size of the habit. Learning how *your* habits work gives you massive edge in your life.

The videos, podcasts, posts, books, and so on, that you will find on alcoholmastery.com and AlcoholMasteryTV on YouTube, are all about guiding you through the basic principles of habit formation and habit breakdown. But they can only take you so far. Only you have the ability to adapt those principles to yourself and the habits in your life. You are the only one who has the deep understanding of your own habits, of what makes them unique. You are also in the best position to truly understand where you want to go in your life, how you're going to get there, and to give yourself the best motivations to get the job done.

Real Time Adjustments

Your habits play out in real time. Every moment of every day your habits are moving through their sequences. You have a ringside seat. It's up to you to observe each thought as it happens. As each trigger is sparked off, you know about it immediately. Only you have an all-areas-access-pass to your every sound, sight, feeling, taste, or smell that goes on inside your being. This means that only you are in the best place to adjust in real time, eliminating some triggers or encouraging others, depending on which direction you want each habit to take.

Your habits don't discriminate by morals, ethics, benefits, or harm. They only respond to repetition. If you do something over and over again, you *will* turn it into a habit. Once you stop repeating the actions, you break the habit cycle. This is why real time habit adjustments work so well. You break the habit in real time, chipping away at it bit by bit, until there is nothing left but a habit memory.

Believing Passionately

I am a great believer in the Law of Attraction. I'm not talking about the quite unusual belief that there's a force in the universe enabling you to make things appear in your life through some universal karmic influence. I don't know if that power exists, maybe it does, but I don't really care. That's completely out of my control.

A more realistic version of the Law of Attraction is that *you are what you think you are.* You control your thoughts and by controlling your thoughts you control your actions. What you think about yourself will always define who you are. The thoughts you have about your abilities to achieve in life are only ever as strong as the limits you set for yourself. If you believe you cannot do something, the chances are you will not do it. Your self-belief is what makes everything possible.

Nikos Kazantzakis, author of *Zorba the Greek*, said, "By believing passionately in that which does not yet exist, you create it. The non-existent is whatever we have not sufficiently desired."

Everything we will ever do must start life with a thought. The most fantastic and complex achievements of mankind, from landing a man on the Moon to saving the life of a premature baby, first had to be a single thought inside the mind of a single human being.

You need to understand that this addiction is not about the alcohol. It's not about this evil thing that is hell-bent on taking control of your life. It's all about you, your thoughts, perceptions, habits, self-concept, self-belief, and how you interpret your background and your culture. Looking at your life from this self-determined perspective gives you the ability to change anything.

Living Your Life Like A Scientist

"All life is an experiment. The more experiments you make the better."
Ralph Waldo Emerson

What Happens If...?

We are all born as scientists. We explore, we test, we adjust and test some more. We want to see what happens if...! What happens if I put my finger in there? What happens if I jump into that puddle? What does this taste like? Will it taste different if I put it into my mouth the other way around? What happens if I put one foot in front of the other? What happens if I do it faster?

When we are young, we are excited to perform a seemingly never ending stream of experiments. Unfortunately, this type of experimental behavior is only tolerated until a certain age. Then we are forced to sit still, not to ask silly questions, and to just accept that which we have been told.

It's time for you rediscover your inner scientist, to ask what happens if ... ?

Try, Fail, Learn, Adjust...

Nothing works for everyone except experimentation. As long as you are always willing to experiment, to try and fail, you will always figure out what works for you. What works for me, and a billion other people, might not work for you. If you find that something is not working the way you expected, don't give in. Sometimes all it takes is for you to make a little tweak here and there to re-purpose these mindsets and principles so that work for you.

The sequence for experimentation is simple:

Try→Learn→Adjust→
Try→Learn→Adjust→
Try→Learn→Adjust→
... Try→Success!

You keep trying until you find the success! There is no such thing as failure, there are only more opportunities to learn. Each time you try and don't reach success, you examine what you have done, check what went right and what went wrong. Then you run the whole process through again. Each new iteration of the sequence takes into account what you've just learned in the previous iteration. Rinse and repeat! Rinse and repeat! You cannot fail to achieve your new life once you keep trying.

Just as every journey begins with a solitary footstep, so your transformation away from alcohol starts out as a single adjustment. Adjustments are the building blocks for constructing whatever you desire in life. They are the foundation of your success blueprint.

Life Without Alcohol

While you are drinking alcohol, most great things are simply impossible for you because of the wasting nature of this destructive habit. When you are wasting your time thinking about drinking, you are not doing the things you need to do to advance in life. While you are propping up a bar or getting wasted in front of the TV, the opportunity costs of your life are mounting. While you are sleeping off the alcohol, you cannot do the things you need to do to achieve your dreams. While you are spending your time hungover, you cannot spend the time being productive. While your brain is steeped in alcohol, how can you think the great thoughts that create the great values that are going to make your life great!

I used to fear what my life would look like without alcohol. I feared that my life would be empty and hollow. *How will I socialize? Will I lose all my friends? Will I be a miserable bastard forever?*

How naive I was! Now, I fear what my life will become if I ever drank again!

It will not take long for you to understand this very simple truth. Once alcohol is not poisoning your life, you will finally appreciate just how valuable your life is, what you are capable of doing in your life, and your fears will prevent you from ever drinking alcohol again.

I wish you the very best of luck.

Onwards and Upwards!

$5 Discount on How to Stop Drinking Audiobook

As a thank you for purchasing this ebook, here's a discount voucher to get $5 off the audiobook version. Simply go to this link http://selz.co/1GEbezG and enter the code: 89YERPNP in the discount field. You can download and listen to the audiobook instantly... Thank you and enjoy!

Please Leave a Review of This Book on Amazon

Now that you've finished reading *How To Stop Drinking Alcohol*, would you be kind enough to help spread the word by leaving an amazon review.

Your feedback helps keep alcoholmastery.com a free resource. If you loved the book, please let me know :)

To submit a review:
Go to the How to Stop Drinking Alcohol product page on Amazon.com by going here:
http://www.amazon.com/dp/B00MX5DXW2
or Amazon.co.uk by going here:
http://www.amazon.co.uk/gp/product/B00MX5DXW2?*Version*
=1&*entries*=0

Click on the 'Write a customer review' in the Customer Reviews section and write your short review.
Click Submit.

More Information About Quitting Alcohol

If you would like more information about quitting alcohol you can visit our website at: alcoholmastery.com

At the time of writing there are over 300 FREE quit alcohol video tutorials for you to choose from.

You can also listen to our regular podcast on iTunes by visiting iTunes and typing Alcohol Mastery Podcast in the search box.

If you have any questions or topics you would like to see featured on the podcast or in the videos, please contact me. My email is kevin@alcoholmastery.com.

Onwards and Upwards!

Free Alcohol Mastery Newsletter

You can find the Alcohol Mastery free newsletter by going to the website and entering your first name and email address in the box at the top of the home page. I'm looking forward to hearing from you.

Other Books by Kevin O'Hara

Alcohol Freedom - 7 Powerful Mindsets to Kickstart Your Alcohol-Free Journey!

Available on Kindle, Paperback, & Audiobook

(See the next section for a sample chapter)

eBook on Amazon.com by going here:
http://www.amazon.com/dp/B00TYI04UA

Paperback also available on Amazon.com

Alcohol Freedom Sample Chapter Part One

Introduction

Welcome to *Alcohol Freedom, 7 Powerful Mindsets to Kickstart Your Alcohol-Free Journey!* This book is for anyone who wants to quit drinking alcohol but doesn't know how to get started. If that is you, I can understand something of what you are feeling. A little over two years ago, as I write these words, I was in a similar position to the one you are in now. What I've learned in those two years will help you to avoid a lot of unnecessary pain and suffering. If I had only five minutes to speak to you, my message would be simple: You are *not* an alcoholic. You have built a bad habit involving alcohol over many years, but that bad habit can be torn to shreds in a matter of weeks by changing the some of the ways you think. Luckily, because you have bought this book, I have a bit more than five minutes to deliver my message.

I would love to be able to tell you that before I quit drinking alcohol I had this wonderful epiphany, showing me the one way of beating my alcohol habit. It wasn't like that. My drinking had been worrying me for a long time before I finally stopped. For the most part, I had been thinking about how I could cut down. I didn't want to quit. Maybe I could only drink over the weekends, with meals, or while I was watching the football. But I've had these thoughts about restricting my alcohol use enough times to know that I couldn't control anything about my drinking. I'd follow that path for a few weeks, holding tight to my own controls. Then gradually I'd let go a little here, a bit more there, and soon I would be right back where I started: drinking alcohol whenever and wherever I felt like it.

Although I didn't have that initial flash of insight, there *was* one single event that helped to finally make up my mind to quit. I talked about this in my first book, *How to Stop Drinking Alcohol.* I only got to see my son two or three times a year. Each of those occasions was treated like a good old fashioned celebration. In my world, celebrations always meant plenty of food and alcohol. The year I quit, I had just spent over a week 'celebrating' with my son. By the time he returned home, at the end of his vacation, I had spent a small fortune and had no great memories to show for it. In fact, I didn't have many memories. They were all lost to the alcohol smog. Thinking about this in the long term, I realized that every time I met my son in the future would end in similar circumstances. What a crappy way to live. I decided to quit, but I hadn't got a clue *how* I was actually going to do it!

On average, we live about twenty seven thousand days on this planet. Not very many when it's put like that, is it! Since I was a teenager, my alcohol habit had been slowly snipping away at the edges of those twenty seven thousand days. I had already spent a huge block of that time being wasted on booze and I didn't want to waste any more.

When I reached the conclusion that I had to quit for good, I felt frightened and isolated. I was completely ashamed about the person I had become, the drunk or the alcoholic. I felt like a loser. I felt like an outsider in my own world because, as far as I was concerned, I was the only person who had this problem.

I was scared because I wasn't sure if I could have a normal life again. Had I gone too far with my drinking? Would I be able to rise above this and stop using alcohol completely? How long would it take? How would I feel? What damage had I caused to myself? What damage had I caused to my relationships? What would happen to my social life? I had so many questions and not very many good answers.

I imagined that once my 'alcoholism' was made public, people would be talking about me behind my back. I dreaded the humiliation that I would feel every time I had to refuse a glass of wine at a meal or sit watching a football match with an orange juice, while all my buddies were enjoying their ice cold pints of beer.

I felt pissed off and cheated because, once I quit, I would be depriving myself of something that genuinely gave me great pleasure.

It was just a lousy situation to be in. I knew I really needed to stop the destruction. How I was living my life was beyond the joke and there was no way I could hide from the consequences of drinking so much alcohol anymore. But being a drinker still felt like such a natural part of my life, of who I was as a person.

The truth is that when I quit I did feel humiliated. I did feel deprived, and I did feel that some people were talking behind my back, calling me an alcoholic, or worse. That really hurt me. The pitying looks, the jokes, and the remarks were all real and they made me feel like crap. I felt like I had completely let myself and my family down. It almost drove me back to the drink.

But that was in the beginning. Each day that went by without drinking alcohol made my body and mind feel stronger and sharper. The humiliation and the thoughts about being deprived didn't last long because there was no substance behind them. What I realized was that these thoughts were just a part of the drinker's mentality that I had built up over many years. We all get suckered into the propaganda and the lies about how alcohol is a normal part of life. How could I feel deprived when I was feeling happier than I had felt in a very long time. Far from being humiliated, I was elated and raring to go. I knew I had wasted so many years on this pathetic drug, but that all in the past.

The mindsets that I have set out for you in this book will help you to pull back and view your alcohol drinking from a much wider perspective. You will be able to see behavior patterns that other people cannot see. The simplest, easiest, and most efficient way of making changes in your life is by changing the how you think. If you change one aspect of your thinking, that change will have a knock-on effect that can alter your whole life. These changes are simple shifts in your perspective, alternative ways of looking at things.
I'm so excited that you have chosen me to be your guide through this exciting time in your life. These mindsets have changed my life and given me a strong belief in who I am and in my abilities to create my own future. I hope they will do the same for you.

I'm Kevin O'Hara of Alcohol Mastery...

Let's go onwards and upwards!

Alcohol Freedom Sample Chapter Part Two

Alcohol Freedom Mindset One

Quitting Drinking is 5% of What Happens To You and 95% How You Respond

"You can have all the tools in the world but if you don't genuinely believe in yourself, it's useless."
Ken Jeong

You are about to start a new chapter in your life. To stop drinking alcohol is only the first sentence of the first paragraph of that first chapter. The process of quitting alcohol doesn't take years, months, weeks, or even days - it's over in a moment. Imagine stepping through a doorway and closing the door behind you. It's as simple as that. If you decide, right now, *in this very moment*, to never use alcohol again… you've succeeded - Congratulations! You've done it! You've just quit alcohol and there is no more to it than that.

At the heart of any habit, there is a fundamental core that holds the whole structure together. Imagine that your habit is a hot air balloon drifting across the sky. What is it that keeps that balloon from crashing down to earth in a crumpled heap? Heat! A gas burner heats the air inside the balloon, the hot air rises, which takes the surrounding balloon with it up into the atmosphere. If you turn off the burner, thereby taking away the heat source, the whole structure collapses and sinks to the ground.

Building Your Habit

In a similar fashion, any habit is fundamentally built around a single core behavior. A drug habit is built around the behavior of taking a particular drug. A chocolate habit is built around the behavior of eating loads of chocolate. A running habit is built around running. A nose-picking habit is built around picking your nose. A teeth-brushing habit is built around the habit of brushing your teeth. Your alcohol habit is built around your behavior of drinking alcohol. Removing any of these behaviors means that the structure of the habit cannot survive.

Just taking the alcohol out of the habit doesn't mean the habit is gone from your life. There are still going to be companies that make alcohol, places that sell alcohol, advertisements for the various alcohol brands, and other people who drink alcohol. You have no control over any of this. Your control lies in what you put into your body. It doesn't matter how much alcohol there is in the world, if you control the behavior of drinking the alcohol, you'll never have an alcohol problem again. Of course, there are still plenty of other less harmful uses for alcohol. You can use it as a fuel, an industrial solvent, or a cleaner.

So from your point of view, the only thing that's holding your alcohol habit together is not the alcohol, but your alcohol-drinking behavior. This is a major distinction. A person who blames the alcohol is merely deflecting attention away from themselves, from their drinking thoughts, and from the very behavior that lies at the root cause of their problems. The alcohol is merely the tool you use to get the end result you want. If a person stabs someone with a knife, you don't lock up the knife. Blaming alcohol instead of yourself as the drinker means you're likely to stay on the same destructive path.

On the other hand, the person who understands that the entire alcohol habit is structured around the behavior of putting alcohol into their bodies, mouthful after mouthful, can change the entire course of their lives by changing the behavior. Without drinking the alcohol, the habit cannot hold itself together. Just as a hot air balloon cannot stay afloat without heat, the alcohol habit without the alcohol-drinking behavior will collapse.

The Drinking Life Desire

Just as a balloon can be kept afloat by replacing the hot air with another buoyant gas, you can also do a really good job of keeping the structure of your alcohol habit artificially inflated by pumping in a lot of psychological 'hot air'. For instance, you can keep it afloat by telling yourself that you're an alcoholic and you'll never be free from the 'demon drink'. You can tell yourself that alcoholism is in your genes, in your family, or that drinking alcohol is a part of your cultural identity. Even long after the last vestiges of alcohol have disappeared from your system, you can keep the alcohol addiction alive and well through your thoughts and perceptions. Even though the alcohol flow has stopped, the desire for the drinking lifestyle is still strong.

If you don't *want* to quit, you never will, no matter how long you go without actually drinking alcohol. To reach permanent alcohol freedom, you must kill the desire for drinking this toxin. Alcohol Mastery is a free online resource I've set up to help you kill that desire. You can find out more by visiting http://alcoholmastery.com.

Can you recognize that your alcohol habit has been caused by each mouthful of alcohol, that nobody forced you to drink, and that each drink was completely under your control? Are you beginning to recognize that all those changes you now need to make in your life have absolutely nothing to do with the alcohol once you don't drink anymore?

Some people say that they cannot control their drinking, that once they have that first drink in a session, they can't stop. The reality is that once they start, they don't want to stop. There's a big difference between can't and won't.

What to Expect from This Book

This quick introduction to the ideas of   will give you a few simple techniques to dismantle or re-purpose those alcohol habit structures. Once you've worked your way through this book, you will have enough ammunition to begin breaking down those limiting beliefs and values that have brought you to where you are now. You will also learn some skills to begin laying those all-important foundational stones on which you will base all your future success.

These techniques will help you to quickly overcome your alcohol drug habit. They will also help you to effectively deal with any other bad habits that are lurking in the darker recesses of your mind. Additionally, the tools and techniques with which you rid yourself of this bad habit are essentially the same ones that will help you to build the constructive habits that are the foundation of your success.

We all have problems. That's just a part of life. The most common way of trying to solve these problems is to look for easy, external solutions. We often seek out people who can offer us quick fixes that take very little effort on our part. We want a 'buy-now-pay-later' ticket away from our difficulties and into lifelong happiness.

How much would you be willing to pay to get your hands on that one piece of essential advice that would alter your life forever? Or how much would you fork out for a wonder drug that would magically cure all your problems with one simple dose? All you have to do is take the pill, go to sleep, and wake up happy, healthy, with your new life awaiting you. Some of us will read book after book, attend seminar after seminar, searching for that single perfect solution that will lead us to our personal promised land.

If it were that easy, everyone would already be doing it!

On Being Your Own Teacher

ALL the answers to ALL your problems can only really be found inside your own mind. I'm not suggesting that there's a hidden chamber within the deep recesses of your brain, a cerebral Aladdin's cave, where nicely-packaged answers are waiting to be found. We all need help from time to time, but external help will only take you so far.

Outside help is great for opening your mind to other possibilities or giving you a deeper understanding of the best direction for you to take. But any external help - whether in the form of teacher, coach, book, audio, or seminar - can only take you to the threshold of your own problems and no further. External teachings can open you up to a new way of doing things, but they can't take the journey for you. There are a few different reasons for this.

The first reason is that knowledge is not the same as action. You can have all the knowledge in the world, but it's worthless if you don't put it to use. Complete learning means altering your behavior. If your behavior hasn't changed, you haven't learned.

Second, nobody has the same perceptions as you. When someone gives you advice, including what you're reading here, they're teaching you how to do things based upon their perceptions, on how they see things within their own mind. Even if your perceptions are closely matched to those of your teacher, there are still going to be big differences between how your teacher perceives things and how you perceive things. Any advice they give you will have to be adapted to your own way of thinking before you can use it.

Third, not every tool or technique will work for you. One of the answers is to learn many tools and techniques. Another is to learn how to adapt a particular tool or technique so that it fits in with your way of doing things.

Only you can understand yourself with enough insight and intimacy to be able to judge how you can adapt and apply those teachings. You make the adaptations according to your life, your environment, your body, your age, your circumstances, etc. You know if a tool or a technique is working because you receive immediate feedback. You can understand exactly what's happening in real time. You also have the ability to immediately alter the course of your thinking or your actions. By changing the course of your thoughts, you alter your perceptions and control the outcomes.

Now, you might think that you don't know enough about yourself to be able to tell if something is working or not. You might tell yourself that if you understood yourself better, you wouldn't have these problems in the first place. That's just not true. We know ourselves better than anyone else can ever know us. In most cases, all we really lack are the right tools, techniques, or strategies for altering our thinking and perceptions.

Once we learn those tools, techniques, and strategies of change, as well as learn how we can operate them within our own psychology, we can quickly apply them to our thoughts and perceptions. Change your thoughts and perceptions and your actions will largely take care of themselves. Every action first requires a thought. If you control the thoughts, you control the actions.

Your Discomfort Zone

Comfort is one of the biggest enemies of change. We love comfort. It's a basic need and a state we're always pursuing. We seek to gain comfort and avoid pain in most areas of our lives. And we don't like being outside of our zone of comfort for too long. The ability to push yourself over your personal comfort boundary and into your discomfort zone is something only you can do, and it's something that needs to be done if you're serious about making these changes in your life.

As we saw at the beginning of this chapter, your ability to stop drinking both is and is not about the alcohol. Of course alcohol is your initial target because it's been the focus of your behavior for many years. Once you get to the stage of accepting that you need to quit, the alcohol seems to be the barrier that separates you from the life you want.

As soon as you pull the alcohol out of the equation, you realize that it's your thinking that's been the problem all along. The type of thinking you've been doing has resulted in the creation of habitual behavior patterns in your life that are now causing all sorts of problems. Alcohol is merely the means to your end. Now that the alcohol is gone, the whole behavioral structure will start to collapse, leaving gaps that drinking used to fill.

You used to drink after work. Now what? You used to drink when you were stressed. Now what?

A Time for Change

Now is the time for you to turn your back on alcohol and begin to fill those gaps with less harmful behavior. Think about it like a gardener pulling out the weeds and replacing them with strong healthy plants.

The first mindset is about learning a few tools that you can use to alter your thinking and perceptions. These early tools are not going to change your life, but they'll be just enough to get you over that starting line.

Once your brain has had the chance to remain alcohol-free in the first few days, alcohol can't influence your thoughts any more or interfere with those delicate chemical and electrical balances that are so essential for a fully functioning mind. Once these chemical and electrical connections are functioning properly, your thoughts and perceptions will become clearer. Your new cleaner-running brain will be much more productive, positive, and capable. Each day that goes by gives you more experience of what it's like to be free.

Getting your head in the right place means choosing how you are going to think, how you are going to react, and how you are going to feel. It means putting yourself in the driver's seat once again. You will be in complete control.

In the next section, we're going to examine some of the more common assumptions about alcohol consumption and quitting.

For more, you can buy Alcohol Freedom on Amazon.com.

Printed in Germany
by Amazon Distribution
GmbH, Leipzig

20571250R00107